let me fall

let me fall

the love story between God and His dimwitted daughter

• BETH PENSINGER •

Let Me Fall: The Love Story Between God and His Dimwitted Daughter

Published by Peracto Books, LLC
P.O. Box 162, Conway, SC 29528
Copyright © 2013 by Beth Pensinger

All rights reserved. Published 2013. No portion of this book may be reproduced, stored in a retrieval system, or transmitted in any form or by any means—electronic, mechanical, photocopy, recording, or any other—except for brief quotation in printed reviews, without the prior permission of the publisher.

All real names used with permission. Remaining names have been changed for privacy purposes.

The web site addresses referenced in the Notes are not intended in any way to be or imply an endorsement on the part of Peracto Books, LLC, nor do we vouch for their content.

Unless otherwise indicated, all Scripture quotations are from the *Holy Bible*, English Standard Version® (ESV®), copyright © 2001 by Crossway, a publishing ministry of Good News Publishers. Used by permission. All rights reserved. Italics in Scripture quotations have been added by the author for emphasis. Scripture quotations marked NKJV are taken from the New King James Version® copyright © 1982 by Thomas Nelson, Inc. Used by permission. All rights reserved.

Lyrics to *You Would Love Me Too* reprinted with permission. Copyright © 2009 Jennifer Heller, David Heller/Butter Lid Publishing (ASCAP)

Quote from Dr. L. Douglas Dorman used with permission. Copyright © 2011 Your Next Step Ministries

ISBN: 978-0-9890684-0-6
Library of Congress Control Number: 2013903825

Cover Design: Soheil Tousi, 2013
Author Photo: Hannah Lockaby, 2012

Printed in the United States of America

How have I put God in a box? More importantly, how do I get Him out of said box?

Journal Entry, May 23, 2009

Abba,

By Your grace and for Your glory, I will write *Let Me Fall* and get it published even though I'm weak and full of fear.

Love,
Beth, April 14, 2010

• Contents •

• Preface •

I hesitate to probe into the dark chasms of my life. The more of my innards I expose, the more dysfunctional and grotesque I feel. Baring my soul for the price of a book is a difficult thing to do.

So why bother? Well, maybe I'm not the only one to experience such dark chasms. And maybe baring my soul will result in someone else's emotional gain.

There are some thoughts so well said they need not be expanded upon. And while I did not come up with the statements penned below, these two sum up the way I feel about *Let Me Fall.*

> This book is a modest attempt to aid God's hungry children so to find Him. Nothing here is new except in the sense that it is a discovery which my own heart has made of spiritual realities most delightful and wonderful to me. Others before me have gone much farther into these holy mysteries than I have done, but if my fire is not large it is yet real, and there may be those who can light their candle at its flame.
>
> From the preface to
> *The Pursuit of God*, A.W. Tozer[1]

O to grace how great a debtor
Daily I'm constrained to be!
Let Thy goodness, like a fetter,
Bind my wandering heart to Thee.
Prone to wander, Lord, I feel it,
Prone to leave the God I love;
Here's my heart, O take and seal it,
Seal it for Thy courts above.

Come Thou Fount of Every Blessing,
Robert Robinson[2]

• Chapter 1 •
Let's Start At the Beginning

Anyone who's struggled with an addiction of some sort would agree that finding lasting contentment from the actual addiction is much like a dog chasing its tail—only a lot less adorable.

There is a fire that threatens to consume me. It's kindled by romance, stoked by story, and it burns deep within this idealistic heart of mine. If I had attended an addiction recovery meeting in the spring of 2009, my intro would've gone something like this: Hello, I'm Beth. I'm twenty-eight years old. And although I've been happily married for almost eleven years, I'm obsessed with Stephenie Meyer's *Twilight* series.

"Big deal," you say. "So you like a group of books portraying the romance between a vampire heartthrob and a clumsy human girl. Get over it."

Unfortunately, this fire is much harder to extinguish.

As I pen these words, it's an overcast Coastal South Carolina day. I'm sitting in my tiny home office/guest room with its two long windows open to the world beyond. Though it is dreary out of doors, the cool March air holds the promise of spring. I find myself mentally drawn to the other side of the country, to a place I've only seen in pictures. It's a small town named Forks, nestled within the Olympic Peninsula. And it is in this breathtaking Washington backdrop that my heart was swept up in an epic love story.

This obsession has been a private affair for me. Come to think of it, most obsessions probably *are* private. What I mean is, I feel I've grown to know Bella Swan and Edward Cullen personally, as if they are real flesh and blood (well, at least Bella). Everyone else be warned. Stay away; their love story is mine alone. I am so possessive of it and them, I don't even like verbalizing their names—it seems trite and foolish when so many thousands of women toss them around like romantic mantra.

I am neither Team Edward nor Team Jacob. I am not a Twi-anything. In fact, I detest the cutesy labels with which society brands people and products. I am, however, a lover of all things romantic. And, for me, this may be the quintessential love story.

My obsession didn't begin the moment I read the first book. The gravitational pull toward romanticism began shortly after exiting my mother's womb. I really didn't have a say in the matter. At least not at first.

1985 was a good year. Microsoft released Windows 1.0. The wreckage of the Titanic was discovered in the Atlantic. And my great-grandma turned ninety, which was, of course, cause for family celebration. As a shy five-year-old, I was excited to be at my aunt's house in a new state and caught up in the energy of the adults around me. My two brothers generally didn't want to be bothered by their gum-smacking, doll-toting little sister. But I do remember carousing with my older cousins, Jeremi and Ben, who lived too far away to play with on a regular basis. While I like to think it was my wit and charm, there was really only *one* natural phenomenon that could possibly cause four boys between the ages of seven and eleven to include a girl into their He-Man Woman-Haters Club.

The need for a Princess Leia. (Insert ethereal theme music here.)

Leia wasn't your average princess. Yes, she looked hot in a metal bikini and could rock out a double bun and lip gloss, but there was *so* much more to her intrigue. She was a bold fighter and a spy who knew how to handle a weapon. And, chiefly relevant to this scenario, she took risks. Her daring acts often landed her in need of rescue from the evil clutches of Darth Vader by Luke and Han Solo.

Thus began my afternoon of heroine headlining.

Squealing, I ran from cousin Vader. Even though a pair of spindly, pre-pubescent legs stuck out below his mask and black cape, he still managed to terrify me. I honed in on a hiding spot and scurried for cover. Waiting as patiently as a five-year-old could, my mind wandered to Han. I knew he and Leia were in love. After all, I'd seen the movies. I saw them kiss, which was apparently what people in love did.

I wanted that. But not just the kiss.

There seemed to be something more; something I couldn't quite put my finger on. He looked at her kind of funny, but not in an altogether bad way. And, even though he wasn't looking my way, I found his gaze gave *me* the shivers. In that hiding spot, I waited with eager anticipation for my real-life Han to discover me.

Of course—in the context of the make-believe game—when I was finally found, there was no kiss or anything remotely like it. Han was my cousin, and we're not *that* kind of family! But, I had allowed myself to imagine ... to dream.

Even from a young age, I was hooked. Love intrigued me. Romance lit a fire inside me. I may not have been old enough to understand it, but I knew I wanted to see and experience more.

Fortunately for me, *more* was everywhere I turned. All the Disney princesses found true love. Except Sleeping Beauty. Prince Phillip was a random guy she met once, who fought a purple dragon to get a chance to kiss her. In my opinion, that wasn't much better than their already-arranged marriage. Her prince may have been handsome enough to grace the cover of the cartoon edition of GQ, but he was most likely dumb as a rock. What then? Nobody wants to spend happily ever after with a buffoon. The same went for Cinderella. One dance with the guy then till death do us part? *Really*? Was his worthless attempt to pursue her at the stroke of midnight an impressive display of his character? Humph. *I* certainly didn't think so.

As in Star Wars, my preferred romances were heavy on the flirtatious interaction between hero and heroine. All too soon, the Disney princesses were not enough.

Like a newborn baby eventually craving solid food, my romantic appetite grew with me. More than once my mother questioned my reading the Sweet Valley High series when I was only in middle school. She thought reading about the love lives of high-schoolers might not be a good idea for her impressionable pre-teen. I convinced her it was perfectly fine—mostly stories about babysitting and homework—and gobbled up every rated PG-13 morsel I could.

Up to that point, my addiction had a wholesome aspect to it (if any addiction can be considered wholesome). After all, Sleeping Beauty wasn't actually sleeping *with* Prince Phillip, and the Sweet Valley high couples kept it toned down to first-base.

But teenage break-up drama was nothing compared to what I discovered in high school, when Freshman English entered the scene. My teacher had her own personal library from which we could check out books. I don't know what made me pick up *Honor's Splendor* by Julie Garwood, but pick it up I did. After sauntering over to my teacher's desk, book in tow, I was informed I would have to get my parent's permission to check it out. I didn't know what to expect exactly, but the fact I needed parental sanction was surely a good sign.

My teacher allowed me to bring it home overnight in

order to let my mom peruse it. I didn't cheat either—Mom inspected the book. It was extremely beneficial in my case that the cover didn't have some long-haired, half-naked beauty in the arms of Fabio with an imposing European castle as a backdrop. But this was not the only fact that helped it pass Mom's scrutiny. It was the Bible verse quoted at the top of Chapter 1 that sealed the deal: "Finally, brothers, whatever is true, whatever is honorable, whatever is just, whatever is pure, whatever is lovely, whatever is commendable, if there is any excellence, if there is anything worthy of praise, think about these things." Philippians 4:8[1]

Rarely before had a Bible verse been used so well to pull the wool over someone's eyes. Mom didn't share her thoughts with me, but I'm sure they were something along the lines of: *Good! My daughter must finally want to read about God-centered relationships.*

The truth is, God-centered relationships and I did not even exist on the same wavelength. Romance addiction lovingly grabbed my hand and, together, my constant companion and I skipped toward a new low: explicit sex scenes.

It was pretty powerful stuff. I quickly started my own, private Julie Garwood collection. I didn't have to memorize the page numbers of the enthralling exhibitions because the bindings of each book were well-worn in those locales. It seemed Freshman English and Mrs. Garwood collaborated right under my mom's nose to introduce me to a whole new level of romance. In a figurative nutshell: I officially graduated from 100 Wholesome Street and moved right into the Playboy mansion.

The funny thing is, I would completely justify my dirty reading by reminding myself most of the depicted interludes were between married couples. *I'm not reading about people having torrid affairs. Sex is safe within the confines of marriage—right?* And, at least I wasn't running around *having* sex.

No, I was not. But I had become addicted to *reading* about it.

I could argue that my addiction was not a horribly bad thing. I mean I wasn't hurting anyone, other than myself. I wasn't even hurting myself *physically*. But reading those scenes was like consuming an exquisite dessert and then discovering a weird aftertaste. Naturally, I had to keep eating more and more in order to cleanse my palate of the byproduct—introducing new and exotic flavors one after another.

If someone examined me, they would never have imagined the vivid scenes occupying my thoughts. My life played out as typically as any girl in high school. I tried not to get caught passing notes in class, stressed about finding friends to sit with at lunch, and wrestled with the ongoing question of using both backpack straps so my back wouldn't hurt, or using one strap so I could look cool.

But operating in the real world did not come easy to me. At some point, if I ever wanted to experience this love about which I so desperately dreamt—meeting my Prince Charming in human form—I would need to enter into my *own* romantic venture. I could read all I wanted about the love other people had together, but reading didn't make it my own. And, as hard as I tried, real life was *nothing* like the fairy tales I had scripted in my mind.

My first kiss is a good example. This was a moment I had dreamed about since I witnessed Han Solo envelop Leia in his roguish embrace and feverishly press his lips to hers (sigh). Theirs was a tender, private declaration of their feelings while hiding from the evil Empire aboard the Millennium Falcon. Mine was at age thirteen during recess with my middle-school peers as an audience.

My boyfriend at the time (and I use that term loosely) was Catholic. I remember his religious practice due to his refraining from eating red meat on Fridays for Lent. He did, however, consume dairy products such as cheese. I am one of the greatest cheese fans known to mankind—as long as the taste of cheese is a direct result of my personal and *purposeful* ingestion of it. I say that because, when we kissed, I felt like a pasteurization plant. There is a reason secondhand cheese is not on the menu at any restaurant.

I also wasn't sure why it was dubbed "French kissing." Were the French the only ones to enjoy this exchange of saliva? Because I sure didn't. My boyfriend's slimy tongue stormed the gates of my lips and was attempting to wrestle mine into submission.

Gross.

To be fair, my boyfriend might not have been a bad kisser other than needing a breath mint. It was simply my first exposure to a physical expression of grown-up love—or something like it—which occurred way too early in my life.

At the time, I was utterly crestfallen that my first kiss was such a disappointment. But things like a dismal first kiss can't keep a good romantic down. I bounced back with an alarming vigor. High school and my new-found attachment to explicit reading material ushered in an unrestrained era of male-mania. Sometime during my merry spiral downward, lines blurred, and were crossed. A few disappeared. I engaged in further physical expressions of grown-up love I had no business even knowing about, let alone acting on. Did I *technically* have sex? No. But the actual act of sex isn't the only behavior that can burden someone with a load of regret.

On the emotional side, I became all about the chase. Not me chasing, but being chased. Having a guy in hot pursuit invigorated me. Though almost as soon as I was caught, I would lose interest and break up with the guy, unless he beat me to it. Once caught, there was no more intrigue or excitement. And if my beloved *fictitious* relationships held those elements, why should I settle for second rate in the real world?

Because my relationships were nothing like my novels, I developed a woe-is-me attitude. I was filled with self-pity over the fact no one seemed to understand or love me the way my favorite heroines were loved. Of course I also happened to be a hormone-filled teenager. I had to play the part. After all, aren't torment and misery a requirement in every great love story? What did it matter if the misery was of my own making?

Through it all, I gained some of what I then considered

valuable insight. Here's a journal entry from my senior year I entitled *Lessons Learned*:

1. Guys only want whores. So, unless you feel like joining the club, don't bother.
2. Guys are jerks no matter what age.
3. Guys always want you more when they can't have you.
4. Learn to like yourself, because sometimes you're the only friend you've got.
5. Relationships are meaningless.
6. If you're not beautiful or talented, no one will spare you a second glance.
7. Punch someone in the mouth if they say, "There are other fish in the sea."
8. Advice really is cheap.
9. It's not possible to be friends with a guy after breaking up.
10. Everything ends.

What profound wisdom! I was a cuddly bundle of braces and teenage angst who was apparently having an extremely bad day. But before I give the impression I was a *complete* pathetic, romance-reading-hormonal wretch, I should mention my life also had high points. One of them was a boy named Jerimiah. He was marriage material. No doubt about it. Though I never would've guessed it at the beginning, he ended up being the prince I had waited for my whole life—in human form.

While it *is* true he was a victim of my above-mentioned catch-and-release program, we remained friends through high school. He disproved number nine on my list and, well, almost the remainder of my top ten. We even started dating again at the end of my senior year. And we kept on dating though he was already at college in one town and I was headed to another school four hours away. During my first year of college, our relationship escalated from casual dating to pretty-serious-future-planning.

That very summer, after a tumultuous year of school and a brief break-up, we were married. I was eighteen and he'd just turned twenty. While we were barely old enough not to need parental consent, we somehow managed to get blessing on both sides. But why so early? Why not give it—and ourselves—a few more years? Simple answer: We did what we thought God wanted us to.

I consider it my second palpable glimpse at the character of God.

I had been under the impression that God's M.O. was to squish us human beings into His cookie-cutter mold and place us on the conveyor belt toward the oven called "Life." Same old recipe and baking temperature for everyone: Grow up, go to college, graduate, begin career, get married, produce two-point-five children, become successful in career, retire, tour the country in an RV, buy a house in Florida, then die. Any variation to this life plan was merely the result of a heavenly quality-control incident.

I was glad to be wrong about God. I was also glad to be married to my Prince Charming in the form of Jerimiah.

After we married, I relieved myself of my Julie Garwood collection. I figured reading about other people's sex lives and enjoying one of my own would not mesh. And since I was no longer reading the trashy novels, I believed my all-things-romantic obsession to be a thing of the past.

This was not the case. I was *still* drawn to other people's love stories. A few years into marriage, I went to a chick-flick with my good friend Dana. It was another typical, corny, romantic comedy. After watching this mediocre movie, I felt crummy inside.

The chick-flick stirred up vague yet bitter emptiness. Jerimiah and I had our share of normal marriage issues, but they were just that. Normal. Nothing in our marriage was bad enough to evoke the emotions I was feeling.

I shared my glum sentiment with Dana and we spent the remainder of the ride home trying to figure out how a movie designed to leave you feeling good could have had the opposite effect on me.

As the pages of my married life rapidly turned, the above experience was no longer an isolated incident. Every book or movie involving even a hint of romance left me with the same bizarre despair at its conclusion. Yet I couldn't seem to get enough.

Then came November 28, 2008 and an incident that proved to be my undoing.

It was my twenty-eighth birthday, and the picture progression captured on camera depicted a smiling version of me, getting down to business opening the newspaper-clad gifts on my lap. Being a thoughtful husband, Jerimiah bought me a book he knew I'd enjoy. A book apparently every woman on earth was enjoying at the time.

Twilight.

To me, *Twilight* was nothing more than a teeny-bopper book I never planned on reading. I already felt moronic due to my romance addiction. I didn't want to add *juvenile* to my list of faults. Secretly though, I couldn't wait. It took me all of one day to read.

Dang that Stephenie Meyer! It's like she jumped into my head, plucked out every idealistic romantic whim, and spun them into the most perfect and compelling and wonderful and epic and sweet love story ever told. (It's true that last sentence is a train wreck, but I'm compelled to express how strongly I felt.) With Christmas around the corner, owning the rest of the books in the series was a non-negotiable.

As the New Year set in, I grew comfortable spying on the *Twilight* world. I could slip in unannounced and watch the story unfold as often as I wanted. I could even go a little deeper and personify Bella. After all, where was the harm in that? As Bella, I could be in love with a man who was self-assured and physically unbreakable. And he loved me back.

Not only did I delight in his love, I thrived on it. It's what got me through the countless, endless hours in a day. I craved his attention and his awe. I lived to say and do things to make him love me even more. I found myself guarding my thoughts, only wanting to think things that would please Edward.

Rising early for work on April Fools Day 2009, I groped my way into the master bathroom. I was bleary-eyed from staying up well past midnight the evening before, feeding my obsession. In the midst of massaging toothpaste onto my gums, a thought struck. *Edward is a fictitious vampire.* The toothbrush clattered to the sink as my hands fell limp at my sides and the full implication of the truth washed over me.

I'm not just a moron, I'm psychotic too.

Without warning, the bathroom door was wrenched open. Despair, in its familiar form, strolled in. Only, this time, light glinted off the cold blade in its hand. Despair lunged and attacked. Not wanting to wake Jerimiah in the next room, my face distorted with silent sobs. I hunched over, attempting to block Despair's merciless stabs. But I couldn't. Thick, hot gobs of my soul splattered onto the framed bathroom mirror.

I knew admission alone would not save me from this powerful attack. I could stop embodying Bella Swan, but it wouldn't be enough. My imaginary *Twilight* role-playing was new, but my obsession toward romance in general was not. My soul was in grave danger of bleeding out. Without conscious thought, I moaned a silent plea to God.

Please help me.

No response was immediately forthcoming. I stilled. Maybe Despair mistook me for dead or just got plain-tuckered-out. Either way, it relented.

Unfortunately, with my soul oozing from cruel wounds, I was too weak to care. With toothpaste crusting in the corners of my mouth, I mused about what a lame ending I would have.

Taken out by Despair—of all things.

The cold slate floor was the last thing I saw.

THUMP

I sucked in air and sat straight up, my eyes darting wildly around.

"Whoa, easy there," said the form standing over me. "You're in rough shape."

He was right. I leaned back against the cabinet doors and took a shaky breath. My chest felt like someone had taken a sledgehammer to it.

"Who—who are you and what happened?" I asked.

"You *did* ask for My help," He said, and I gasped with recognition.

"Despair did a number on you." God bent over and began packing up an electronic-looking device. His concerned eyes never left my face. "You spiritually flat-lined."

I wouldn't have if You'd come sooner, I thought, but there was no way I was going to voice that to Him. Even though I was pretty sure He knew I'd thought it. So instead I mumbled, "What the heck is wrong with me?"

"You're not in love with Me."

"I—What?"

"You heard right. The crux of your problem is the fact that you're not in love with *Me*."

I had the audacity to get angry. "Forgive me, but how is it possible to fall in love with someone I *usually* can't see, hear, or touch in the flesh?

He raised an eyebrow and gave a half-smile. "You didn't seem to have a problem doing *exactly that* with a fictitious vampire."

My lips pursed. "Well played," I muttered.

Instead of gloating like I thought He would, He shot me a tender look and remained silent.

My mind was caught up in a swirl of questions. I asked Jesus to come live in my heart back when I was seven years old, but had I ever been intentional about cultivating our relationship? Was falling in love with God really *that* farfetched? Or was this all just an April Fool's Day hallucination?

I didn't know. I looked at my pajamas and couldn't find any trace of the residual soul goo I expected to be there. I suddenly squeezed my eyes shut, certain when I opened them again, God would be gone.

But even with lidded eyes His voice sounded again, and it was loud and clear. This time I recognized it as the invitation it was.

"Fall in love with Me."

Well ... what did I *really* have to lose?

• Chapter 2 •
Story of Stuck

Then he began to invoke a curse on himself and to swear, "I do not know the man." And immediately the rooster crowed. And Peter remembered the saying of Jesus, "Before the rooster crows, you will deny me three times." And he went out and wept bitterly.

Matthew 26:74-75[1]

I don't think I'm giving anything away when I say that Edward and Bella get married in the last book of the Twilight series. Of course, it takes Edward almost a full novel just to *convince* Bella to marry him, but it is not because she didn't love him.

> "Now will you answer a question for me?" ... he asked.
> "Of course," I answered at once, my eyes opening wide with surprise ...
> He spoke the words slowly. "You don't want

to be my wife."

... "That's not a question," I finally whispered.

... "I was worrying about why you felt that way."

I tried to swallow. "That's not a question, either," I whispered.

"Please, Bella?"

"The truth?" I asked, only mouthing the words.

"Of course. I can take it, whatever it is."

I took a deep breath. "You're going to laugh at me." His eyes flashed up to mine, shocked.

"Laugh? I cannot imagine that."

"You'll see," I muttered, and then I sighed. My face went from white to scarlet in a sudden blaze of chagrin. "Okay, fine! I'm sure this will sound like some big joke to you, but really! It's just so ... so ... so *embarrassing*!" I confessed, and I hid my face against his chest again.

There was a brief pause.

"I'm not following you."

I tilted my head back and glared at him, embarrassment making me lash out, belligerent.

"I'm not *that girl,* Edward. The one who gets married right out of high school like some small-town hick who got knocked up by her

> boyfriend! Do you know what people would think? Do you realize what century this is? People don't just get married at eighteen! Not smart people, not responsible, mature people! I wasn't going to be that girl! That's not who I am ..." I trailed off, losing steam.
>
> *Eclipse,* Stephenie Meyer[2]

It surprises me, given Bella's lack of regard concerning her popularity in *every* other scenario, that she would care what anyone else thought about her getting married young. Still, I get where she's coming from. Although she loved Edward with every ounce of her being and wanted to be with him forever, she was afraid if she married him at eighteen, she would *surely* be misunderstood. Someone was bound to see her as unintelligent and irresponsible. And who wants to be mistaken for the village idiot?

Certainly not me.

Unfortunately, like Bella, I tend to care what others think about me (though obviously this didn't stop me from getting married at eighteen). The difference is, I care *way* more than I should. I want everyone to like and respect me; to think I'm pretty. And witty. And—well, I think you know the rest. To top it off, I typically assume I know what other people are thinking about me, which makes for a silly and hazardous relationship combination. Because, figuratively speaking, I'm thoroughly convinced there are people out there who view me as a nitwitted girl wearing a sparkly, purple dunce cap. They believe my main occupation is to skip from meadow to meadow, picking and sniffing daisies while humming a Disney tune. Or at least that's the way they view the person I *aspire to become*, which is why I'm so nervous and self-conscious about actually trying to become her.

Enter: Twinkles.

Twinkles was not the nicest kitty in the litter. She was too aloof to endure any petting—though I did try. She would enthusiastically spring from her hiding spot to claw at my ankles anytime I walked by. But don't let her kitty antics fool you. She was not playful; she was maniacal. Her psychotic behavior was probably due to the torment she endured from the three human children whom she allowed to live with her. Still, I wasn't fond of her.

I encountered Twinkles daily because she belonged to my at-the-time boss. When I was first hired, we worked out of her house. In order to get away from the "office," she and I usually went out for lunch. One summer day, we decided to hit up our favorite Mexican restaurant and load up on cheese quesadillas.

Before leaving, we made sure the house was locked and got in her mini-van via the garage. As we started down the street, something caught my eye. A bundle of white-spotted fur, vaguely resembling a cat, was mashed against the glass door at the front of the house. Suddenly hysterical with laughter, I yelled at my boss to stop the van. I pointed toward an extremely disgruntled Twinkles.

The churlish feline had been inadvertently trapped in the four inch space between the black front door (which got hot to the touch as the day progressed) and full-glass door she always looked out. Twinkles was forced to stand motionless, her back arched, tail sticking straight up. One paw was raised in midair in a frantic attempt to signal us. Because she was stuck sideways, her single glaring eye followed me as far as she could manage while I made my way back inside to arrange her release.

Years later, I recalled the scene and found it still made me laugh so hard I snorted. But as my bouts of amused snorting wound down, I was struck with an alarming thought. In my mind's eye, it wasn't Twinkles' squished form caught between the doors. It was my own. You see, I had been living between two worlds. Just like Twinkles, I was gazing through the glass at where I wanted to be, to a place that called to me. But I couldn't seem to get there of my own accord.

As I was gazing out at my dream world, the door *behind* me suddenly closed shut—tight. There I sat, my paw raised in midair and unable to move, stuck between where I longed to be and where I was coming from. What was it that held me captive? I was lodged between being:

A Moral and Appropriately-Religious Person

And

An All-In Follower of Jesus Christ

Christ Follower. The words used to drop off my tongue like lead weights. In my mind, they equaled a personal death sentence.

But what was dying?

My perceived intellect and credibility, hence the sparkly dunce cap I mentioned earlier.

Look at the facts. I was buying into an existence based on *faith* that there is an unseen, but holy God. And He sent His Son Jesus to die on a cross and be raised from the dead. Sacrificed so that *I*, as well as everyone else who believes He died for them, could have a relationship with *Him*.

God made this heinous sacrifice because sin entered the world and separated Him from all of humanity. This same God happens to have three different identities wrapped up into one Being: God the Father, His son Jesus, and the Holy Spirit. The Holy Spirit took up permanent residence in my heart once I asked Jesus to take over my life, and gave me supernatural abilities in order to live a righteous life and tell others about what He did for them.

And all of this occurred because the astonishing and preeminent God of the universe—the God who created and weaved something out of nothing—cares about insignificant ... little ... me.

Right. Santa Claus is also my uncle, and every year my family competes in a clandestine reindeer Iditarod at the North Pole. While we're on the subject of delusions, maybe werewolves *are* real and Edward *did* turn Bella into a vampire after she nearly died giving birth to their half-breed spawn.

When you break it all down, following Jesus Christ doesn't make a lick of sense to a lot of rational and intelligent people. Heck, there are quite a few astute minds that don't even make it to *Jesus*. The claim of an all-powerful creator-God stops them dead in their tracks.

With these hang-ups constantly in mind, my problem was presuming that the intelligent people of the world would mock me for my beliefs. They would scorn my lifestyle if I lived like an all-in follower of Jesus Christ because that way of life grates too strongly against the grain of today's society. I feared that all they would see when they looked at me on life's stage is a girl in a worn orange bike helmet, playing the harmonica and singing non-melodiously. Much like a man I once knew named Dudley.

Dudley attended the Friendship Group at the church I went to when I was young. The Friendship Group hosted mentally-handicapped adults. Every so often, Dudley was asked to sing during the church service before the pastor came on stage to do his thing. Dudley was blind and typically wore the above mentioned orange bicycle helmet. Every time he sang, he angled his unfocused gaze up and rocked his large frame back and forth. In a coarse, booming voice he sang a cappella "Jesus, Jesus, Jesus. There's just something about that name." Between choruses, he brought out his harmonica and played a few bars of music.

I am ashamed to admit that, in my adolescent immaturity, I made fun of him. I can be cruel, even if that cruelty only takes place in my head. I was also embarrassed *for* him. I would cringe when I saw him climb up on stage because he was again putting himself out there for treacherous people like me to snicker at. It was uncomfortable for me to watch.

Eventually, though, I recognized the hot and glaring lights from the stage of my own life pointing down at me. I took a hard look at myself and realized something: because of my fear of being ridiculed and pitied the way I did Dudley, I was stuck. I was behind the glass, looking out at a life of truly following Christ, but never able to move into action. I can admit *now* that I was a coward. I think I actually could've been called the Queen of All Wusses.

I revered the *idea* of loving God. I certainly requested it often. Out of all the entries in my adolescent journal, 65% of them included pleas to God, petitioning for His assistance to help me fall in love with Him (yes, I actually did the math). At the same time, I wanted to keep any kind of relationship with Jesus on the down low. I mean *real* low.

I couldn't have the intellectuals and social elites out there thinking reprehensibly of me. I didn't want to say anything that would go against what they accepted as truth, because I was too simple-minded and tongue-tied to engage in any sort of religious debate, friendly or otherwise. Plus, I couldn't prove everything I believed.

So I clamped my mouth shut and firmly established my position as Queen of the Wusses. Long live the Queen. I cowered at the mere thought of man's disdain. I cared little about what *God* thought of the person I was becoming. My actions were living proof that He wasn't as real or important to me as the people I revered.

But, after a while, I was finally called out, much like the Gospel of John called out my invertebrate counterparts of two thousand plus years ago.

> Nevertheless, many even of the authorities believed in him (Jesus), but for fear of the Pharisees they did not confess it, so that they would not be put out of the synagogue; for they loved the glory that comes from man more than the glory that comes from God.
>
> John 12:42-43[3]

Ouch! The truth hurt as bad as the time I slipped on wet concrete at a restaurant entrance and ate pavement in front of a bunch of people I didn't know. Thankfully, God—much like Edward with Bella—didn't stop asking for my hand because of my initial response, or the underlying *reasons* for that response.

• • •

Still lodged between the two doors of reality, my thoughts are interrupted as I see Jesus approach.

He is breathtakingly radiant, majesty rolling off Him in waves. His beautiful voice forms a familiar invitation: "fall in love with Me." He studies my face as I grope for words. Reading *something* in my eyes, He reaches out a hand and opens the glass door for me. After depending on those two doors to hold me upright for so long, the release sends me tumbling onto the ground at His feet.

As I scramble to right myself, I notice the ground is rocky and sprinkled with giant boulders. Confused, I look around and gasp at the new landscape. Apparently there is a lot more on the other side of the glass than I ever imagined, because Jesus and I are standing together near the edge of a great cliff. I'm not talking about the rock wall I might find at a mall. I'm talking a sheer precipice unlike any I have ever seen.

As I continue to scan my new altitude, I notice a rough, wooden sign mounted to a post just before the cliff's edge. I walk closer, tracing the carved letters with my fingers. It reads "To Love God." Beneath those intriguing words, a thick arrow points down. Surely it doesn't mean what I think it does.

Downward? As in, to fall in love with God, I must go over the edge?

I inch closer to the brink while stretching my neck like a giraffe, trying—and failing—to see the bottom. *Sheer craziness!* Just thinking about stepping out into the endless space in front of me causes my vision to blur and my breath to come in short, panicky gasps.

I instinctively shuffle backward until I bump into something solid. This obstacle makes no sense to me, but I am unwilling to turn my back on the distressing edge in front of me in order to investigate. My hands slide over a smooth surface. One comes to rest on a cold metal knob. In my peripheral vision, I make out the unlatched glass door the Lord just opened. So what did I collide with?

The other door! The one that was shut tightly behind me. I must have backed into it. Momentarily forgetting my fear of the edge, I whirl around to examine it. A sign is posted on this door. "Your Life Up Until Now."

I stare blankly at the words. Then re-read them.

So ... these are my choices? Either throw myself off a cliff in the attempt to fall in love with God, or go back the way I came? Back to being a spineless but acceptably religious person?

This is seriously messed up.

Jesus stands a few feet away and I brave a look at Him. He is focused on me but wears an inscrutable expression. *No help there,* I think—annoyed.

So I do the next logical thing. I twist the doorknob. Finding it unlocked, I open wide the door to my old life. It is not like I remembered. Everything my eyes touch is dull and listless.

I start violently when I lock eyes with Despair. It stands only twenty yards past the threshold and holds a knife still covered in my soul-goo. It makes no move toward me, but I hear it whisper, "You'll never be rid of me."

I'm really not sure how long I stand there, transfixed by Despair's haunting voice. Or how many times I nervously pace between the open door to my past and the edge of my potential future.

Jesus' rich voice breaks through my inner strife. "Have you decided yet?" I snap out of my deliberation and focus on His face.

"What's that?" I ask.

He nods toward the dizzying edge. "You've been eyeing that rim for some time now." A smile spreads on His face. "You've actually gotten a small cardiovascular workout from the sheer number of times you've crept toward the edge then backed off." Amusement is evident in His tone. "At the rate you're going, you'll be dancing this little jig for the rest of your life."

I stammer, "I—I know." Then I hesitate. "I just don't think I'm ready to leap yet."

"All right." His words come slowly and his eyes look straight into mine. "What are your concerns?"

"Are You seeing the same edge I am?" I jab my finger out in the direction of the edge. "I'd be *crazy* to step off it. Seriously!" I breathe out with a sarcastic laugh. "As a matter of fact, I think You should demand a full refund from the idiot sign maker who screwed up the direction of the arrow!"

Without missing a beat He says, "Whoever finds his life will lose it, and whoever loses his life for my sake will find it."[4]

I am instantly appalled. "But ... but ... You ask for so much—*too* much!" My voice raises an octave. "Lose my *life*?"

"If anyone comes to me and does not hate his own father and mother and wife and children and brothers and sisters, yes, and even his own life, he cannot be my disciple."[5]

I shake my head in disbelief. "Why would You want that? Me hating my family, everyone I care about? That's horrible!"

"That's not the only instance of Me using hyperbole in that day and age," He says, and seeing my confused look goes on to explain further. "Surely you've overstated something to prove a point."

He waits for my nod then continues. "Simply put, I need to take precedence over all relationships in your life—it's essential that *I* become your main priority. Your main love." He pauses. "I never said that loving Me would be easy. I *am* demanding—I want *all* of you."

I wince as I absorb His words. "I don't know if that's realistic ..." I trail off as I suddenly recall Him mentioning something about being His disciple. "Hold up. Slightly new thought. What's being Your disciple got to do with anything?" I envision a crusty, bearded, middle-aged man adorned in fisherman's garb circa 27 AD.

Jesus grins wryly as if discerning my thoughts. "Look up the definition of disciple."

I whip out my iPhone and let my thumbs loose on the screen. I actually have a signal. Strange. A few moments later I rattle off my findings. "It's a noun that means a person who is a pupil." I skim a little further. "If used in the sense of the Greek verb *manthano*, it implies not just one who follows teaching but also imitates the teacher." I frown as soon as my oral summary is complete. "So ... I'm supposed to *copy* You," I remark flatly.

"Which you're not happy about," He observes.

I raise my chin indignantly and speak in clipped sentences. "Well no. Now that You mention it. I guess I'm not." I pause, feeling defiant. "Fine. I'll say it." I cross my arms and raise one eyebrow. "I don't think I'll like who I'd become. I'm rather fond of *me*."

Jesus lets out a huge sigh. "And just who do you think you'll turn into?"

I commence with my laundry list. "Well ... for starters, an uptight, stuffy, Little House on the Prairie-dressing, WWJD bracelet wearer. I'll become a serious person because of all Your rules and never do anything fun or laugh again, which will be made worse by the fact that I'll only be able to listen to Petra and watch movies and read books that have Amish-looking women on the cover! Next thing I know, You'll want me to start acting like the people on The 700 Club, possibly wanting me to sport big hair and blue eye shadow. The worst part is, I think You'll be displeased with me until I sell everything I have and move to a foreign country wherein I share Your love with the most hostile tribe I'm able to locate!" I gasp for air.

A roar of amusement erupts from His lips and His snorting laughter continues for several long moments. "Oh," He manages between breaths, "is that all?"

"It's not funny!" I reply indignantly, though I feel the corners of my mouth twitch upward.

As His hilarity subsides, He regards me tenderly. "Beth, by becoming My disciple, you'll be imitating *Me*." He teases, "And can you really picture Me sporting big hair and blue eye shadow?" He becomes earnest. "The more you discover about Me, the more you'll realize that I am *not* the sum of all those fears. But first you must—you simply *must*—stop trying to love Me on your own terms." He shakes His head sadly. "It will never work."

"What do You mean?" I ask, my voice barely audible.

He exhales deeply then narrows His eyes thoughtfully at me. "Why don't you tell Me what you're *really* concerned about. No more surface rationale."

I look away for a moment, then back to His face. "Okay.

I'll shoot straight with You." I grimace. "You're not necessarily the ..." I clear my throat and look at my feet. "... popular choice." I bring my eyes back to His. "I'm really scared other people will think I'm either weird or crazy for following You. And I'm pretty sure I'll get made fun of and rejected."

I see a glimmer of deep hurt in His clear gaze as He says, "You can't have it both ways. You can't fall in love with Me and pretend I don't exist to everyone else."

With His last words, hot, shameful tears well up, threatening to spill down my cheeks. "What if I don't have what it takes?" I croak in a shaky voice. "I'm sorta ... spineless." I look down again and study my shoes. "I quite literally am the Queen of—"

He cuts me off. "All Wusses? That's not how I see you." He reaches for me, pulling my chin up so I can meet His gaze. "Have you ever heard of Corrie ten Boom—the Dutch woman whose family hid Jews during World War II and was sent to a concentration camp as a result?" Seeing my nod, He continues. "She *got* it. She was quoted as saying, 'If I had ever needed proof that I had no boldness or cleverness of my own, I had it now. Whatever bravery or skill I had ever shown were gifts of God—sheer loans from Him of the talent needed to do a job.'"[6] He studies my face. "Your life will become a lot easier the moment you begin to rely on Me and not on what are actually your shortcomings. In fact, 'For by grace you have been saved through faith. And this is not your own doing; it is the gift of God, not a result of works, so that no one may boast.'"[7]

"Oh," is all I can think to say.

"Listen to My words again ... 'If anyone would come after me, let him deny himself and take up his cross and follow me. For whoever would save his life will lose it, but whoever loses his life for my sake will *find* it.'[8] You've only focused on what you perceive you'll *lose* by following Me—"

"Instead of what I'll *gain*," I finish. "Wow. When You put it that way ... I feel moderately stupid."

"I forgive you, so you can save yourself the guilt trip." He tucks a wayward strand of hair behind my ear. "You haven't been ready to listen or you would've gotten it long ago watching Dudley."

A goofy grin spreads on my face. "Dudley? From the Friendship Group? Um ... what did I miss?"

He gets a far-off look and smiles. "I gave him the most wondrous gift." He looks pointedly at me. "And *you* had the opportunity to see it in action. Only, you misunderstood it and pitied him instead."

My eyes scrunch as I'm still baffled. "What was his gift? His organ-playing skills? I mean he was quite good at—"

"I don't make mistakes," He says as He gently interrupts me. "I created him exactly the way I wanted him to be."

I gasp in shock. "That seems just plain mean! All the things he never got to do—the challenges he had to live with ... people like *me* treating him with a mixture of ridicule and pity ..." I trail off, dumfounded. "I can't believe You're admitting this to me!"

Jesus shakes His head back and forth emphatically. "In his simplicity, he wasn't forced to conquer the barriers that you're forced to conquer in order to fall in love with M... only see his deficiencies. But I know the full extent of what he's been *given*. His "handicap" actually freed him. He heard My invitation, responded with a *yes*, and worshiped Me unabashedly with the rest of his life. Do you think he *ever* worried about meeting the status quo? Or what other people thought of him?"

I am quiet for several long moments. "I see what You're saying. I guess I'm—what's the word? Humbled." I heave a great sigh. "All my worrying over other people's opinions of me seems rather childish." I mutter to myself, "And fairly non-important considering what You're offering."

"I'm glad you feel that way," He says.

I give Jesus a brief smile and slowly walk back to the still-open door of my past. Leaning in, I grab the knob, engage the lock, and pull the door shut tight, effectively sealing off my former days. I turn toward the cliff and square my shoulders. Adrenaline surges through my body as I think of what I'm about to do.

"Well," I say, as my heart threatens to beat out of my chest, "I'm off." I gulp as I look at the brim of the precipice. "I think I'm finally ready."

"Beth!" He cries with delight and puts a hand on my arm to stop me from moving toward the edge of the cliff. "Do you have *any* idea how much I love you?"

He pulls off a formidable-looking backpack I hadn't noticed before. I watch as He gathers supplies from the pack then securely ties a series of ropes to a massive boulder behind us.

His declaration warms my heart, but I am confused when He places a harness in front of my feet, helps me step into it, and makes adjustments so it fits snugly.

"What—what are You doing?" I ask.

His answering grin is mischievous. "You didn't think I expected you to step off this ledge alone. Did you?"

• Chapter 3 •
A Most Unpleasant Introduction

Narcissist: psychoanalytic term for the person who loves himself more than his analyst; considered to be the manifestation of a dire mental disease whose successful treatment depends on the patient learning to love the analyst more and himself less.

Thomas Szasz[1]

There are people in my life I plain like. They have unique personalities and play different roles in my world. This feels a bit awkward to write, but my gynecologist is one of those people. He is well-respected in the community. Several of my friends as well as their children were brought into the world thanks to his delivery skills. I am drawn to and appreciate his intelligence and quick wit (and if it's not already obvious, I love humor). He makes me laugh and not feel so self-consciously awful about the uncomfortable intricacies all women face during our joyous annual visits with the GYN.

I usually see my doctor once a year and on occasion at church. But one day, I ran into him at the gym. So naturally, when I saw him, I stuck out my hand, shook his, and said, "Hey, it's Beth Pensinger." I was sure he would experience name-amnesia in front of me. He's had a large number of patients over the years. After all, who am I? I'm not big around town. There's nothing especially notable about me. And I have no distinguished status among his practice or family. It is not like I'm invited to Thanksgiving dinner. In his world, I am completely forgettable.

I saw him a few weeks later for my exam. After the exam was over and the doc and I were sitting in his office, he said "Next time you see me at the gym, you don't need to introduce yourself. I know who you are."

Oh really? You do?! I got a weird ego boost from his statement. A man I respect and also consider hilarious knew *my* name without my chart as his guide. I must have made some sort of good impression. He only sees me once a year for crying out loud! *Does he think I'm sweet? Or maybe he believes me to be witty and intelligent.* I was in full peacock mode.

But before my mental glory over the doctoral recognition seems like an isolated incident, I must confess to more.

My husband works for a church. A lot of people who attend know me because they know Jerimiah. I find I rather enjoy his micro-cosmic celebrity status as a church staff member. I've often walked around on Sunday mornings preening my invisible peacock feathers. My internal dialog sounds a lot like: "Ooh, look at me. My husband is important here. We've helped *start* this church."

My silent monologues are disgusting and I am ashamed to let anyone else in on my private struggles. But I do have a reason for exposing my plumage.

I am about to make a statement that might be disputed. I have no scientific proof. I'm certainly no expert. I have not spent years studying the topic, nor written a dissertation on the subject. Regardless of these truths, here it is:

I believe every human who has ever existed and will ever exist suffers from a degree of narcissistic personality disorder (NPD).

I am not *intentionally* trying to offend people with my statement. Nor am I trying to suggest that good and moral people are like history's more infamous narcissists: Nero, Hitler, or the literary character Dorian Gray. And though I'm not sure if my admission will soothe the wound of unintentional offense, I confess to being a narcissist as well.

Let me first attempt to define narcissism.

After comparing the symptoms of narcissism with those of narcissistic personality disorder—or NPD—I failed to notice a worthwhile difference; hence my interchangeable usage of the two terms. This noun means having an inordinate fascination with oneself; excessive self-love; vanity.[2] Though I am not sure exactly who gets to define excessive when it comes to loving one's self.

According to the Mayo Clinic, "Narcissistic personality disorder crosses the border of healthy confidence and self-esteem into thinking so highly of yourself that you put yourself on a pedestal. In contrast, people who have healthy confidence and self-esteem don't value themselves more than they value others." The following are symptoms of NPD per the Mayo Clinic Staff.

Narcissistic personality disorder symptoms may include:

- Believing that you're better than others
- Fantasizing about power, success, and attractiveness
- Exaggerating your achievements or talents
- Expecting constant praise and admiration
- Believing that you're special and acting accordingly
- Failing to recognize other people's emotions and feelings
- Expecting others to go along with your ideas and plans
- Taking advantage of others
- Expressing disdain for those you feel are inferior
- Being jealous of others
- Believing that others are jealous of you
- Trouble keeping healthy relationships
- Setting unrealistic goals
- Being easily hurt and rejected
- Having a fragile self-esteem
- Appearing as tough-minded or unemotional[3]

I'm in trouble. According to the Mayo Clinic's symptoms list, I need to get to a mental health specialist as soon as possible and begin my psychotherapy treatments. Out of the sixteen symptoms listed, I've expressed at least twelve, and some on a regular basis. I'm not going to get hung up on the fact that a lot of these expressions never make it *outside* my mind in the form of words or actions. One exception is my primping, flexing, and face examination nearly every time a mirror is in close proximity. Otherwise, I alone am privy to the daily dialog occurring in my mind; a witness to the unseen crimes committed.

Exhibit A: Eugenia. My first real job was as a receptionist for a church. Eugenia frequented the church. To put it mildly, she was difficult to love. She sometimes had wicked bad breath and was the polar opposite of the phrase "easy on the eyes." She was the female version of Napoleon Dynamite describing his summer in Alaska with his uncle, where he shot "like fifty wolverines" in order to protect his cousins. Eugenia would say severely exaggerated and outlandishly stupid things to which I had no clue how to respond.

Nobody liked Eugenia. People avoided her because she was like a puppy looking for a new human best friend. If you showed her the least bit of interest, she would *never* leave you alone.

But, being the receptionist, I couldn't escape her. So I decided to make the best of it. I asked God to give me a genuine love for Eugenia so I wouldn't have to fake it anymore. I felt *good* for asking Him that. So righteous! The thought crossed my mind that loving her might start with me actually praying for her and any issues she faced. I quickly discarded the idea though. It would feel too unnatural to pray for someone I didn't really care about. It would be a waste of my prayers.

And then my depravity struck me full-force. In my eyes, Eugenia was disposable, a non-person because of the traits I saw as her shortcomings. She was not even worthy of my time.

This way of thinking and reacting to others is second nature to me. But believing I'm better than others and expressing disdain for those I feel are inferior are not the only symptoms I exhibit. Jealousy is another big one. It is my close companion. It radiates from my core and spreads insidiously to every nerve ending in my body.

Mason Cooley said that "the narcissist enjoys being looked at and not looking back."[4] I consider myself pegged. As stupid as it may sound, this is an accurate description of my Facebook experience: I'm usually only on it to post what I believe are witty or deep thoughts meant to generate comments that will boost my self-esteem. I don't spend half the same amount of time checking out my friends' pages.

I'm so into being looked at, I sometimes pretend my life is like the movie *The Truman Show,* starring Jim Carrey. The world watches my every move with rapt attention. Except when I'm going to the bathroom, showering, or making myself look stupid. Okay, that would actually cut out at least half my life.

Thoughts of me are the driving force behind who I am. I love my husband and family—in large part because of the way they make *me* feel. I enjoy being sweet and doing things for others because it makes *me* feel good about *myself*. I can't seem to escape my selfishness.

It's like the *Friends* episode, "The One Where Phoebe Hates PBS," when Joey tells Phoebe there are no unselfish good deeds. She tries the entire show to prove him wrong but ends up feeling good about herself with each good deed. She thinks she has him in the end when she pledges $200 to a PBS telethon Joey is working. Since she hates PBS, her pledge means she completed a selfless act which makes her unhappy. But her pledge ends up earning Joey some on-air camera time. Which makes her feel good about herself.

Just because I am making public my private crud doesn't mean that I'm okay with any of it. I am bothered by my narcissism and can't help but wonder how on earth I ended up this way. Help me, Mayo Clinic ...

> "It's not known what causes narcissistic personality disorder. As with other mental disorders, the cause is likely complex. Some evidence links the cause to a dysfunctional childhood, such as excessive pampering, extremely high expectations, abuse or neglect. It's also possible that genetics or psychobiology—the connection between the brain and behavior and thinking—plays a role in the development of narcissistic personality disorder."[5]

Dysfunctional childhood huh? Well, I am the baby of the family *and* the only girl. That's a fact that *could have* resulted in ponies and over-the-top princess parties. However, I cannot charge my parents with excessive pampering. I got a pair of baby-blue Bongo jeans and ankle-high Eastland boots only *after* they went out of style. Trends become surprisingly affordable once they've disembarked from the fashion train. I didn't have a cell phone in high school because roaming charges on Dad's bag phone were as much as one semester of college. My first car was a hunk of rusting scrap metal that was impossible to get into first gear. Plus I contributed half of the $500 purchase price from my summer job savings.

To exonerate my parents, I must note they were in no way, shape, or form abusive. Being grounded numerous times does not warrant calling Child Protective Services. They were not neglectful. I'm sure at times in my adolescence they were involved a little *too* much for my liking. And, while they did demand a high standard from me, I never felt the pressure of unrealistic expectations from Mom or Dad. Dang it! I must rule them out as being the originators of my narcissism.

So who's to blame?

Other evidence points to "genetics ..."[6]

Meaning I was born a narcissist? Which would still technically be my parents' fault, though unintentional. I'm going with that one. I think it *is* genetics. But I can trace it back well-beyond my great-granddaddy on my mother's side. Try Adam and Eve and the introduction of a short word that has ravaged mankind.

Sin.

The word itself reveals its very nature: 'I' at the center.

Every transgression has self-interest at its foundation having an inordinate fascination with self; excessive self-love; vanity.

> To be specific, the self sins are these: self-righteousness, self-pity, self confidence, self-sufficiency, self-admiration, self-love and a host of others like them. They dwell too deep within us and are too much a part of our natures to come to our attention till the light of God is focused upon them.
>
> *The Pursuit of God,* A.W. Tozer[7]

The psychoanalytic geniuses of our time are attempting to call sin a personality disorder. I can see why. To dub narcissism as sin is to put us on the same playing field as the likes of Hitler. It's much easier to slough off our misbehavior as an accidental genetic anomaly than to admit that we have something in common with an evil monster: sin. We'd like to think only truly sick people are capable of such depravity.

But my argument is that we are all depraved.

Truth doesn't cease to be true just because we call it by another name. Bella said it best in *New Moon:* "What if you sincerely believed something was true, but you were dead wrong? What if you were so stubbornly sure that you were right, that you wouldn't even consider the truth? Would the truth be silenced, or would it try to break through?"[8]

In my case, the painful truth has finally begun to surface. But where do I go from here? A.W. Tozer said, "Self is the opaque veil that hides the Face of God from us. It can be removed only in spiritual experience, never by mere instruction."[9] I do not wish to continue down my narcissistic path. But am I ready to have the veil torn from my face?

> Let us remember: when we talk of the rending of the veil we are speaking in a figure, and the thought of it is poetical, almost pleasant; but in actuality there is nothing pleasant about it. In human experience that veil is made of living spiritual tissue; it is composed of the sentient, quivering stuff of which our whole beings consist, and to touch it is to touch us where we feel pain. To tear it away is to injure us, to hurt us and make us bleed. To say otherwise is to make the cross no cross and death no death at all. It is never fun to die. To rip through the dear and tender stuff of which life is made can never be anything but deeply painful. Yet that is what the cross did to Jesus and it is what the cross would do to every man to set him free.
>
> *The Pursuit of God,* A.W. Tozer[10]

• • •

Jesus and I stand on the bottomless vertical precipice. I walk closer to the edge of the cliff, stare down, and stretch my arms up over my head. I then grab one ankle at a time, pulling each leg into an individual stretch. Once complete, I clap my palms together and rub them back and forth.

"Alrighty then Lord, I'm ready—let's do this thing!" Not hearing a response, I twist to locate Him. "Are *You* ready?"

Jesus nods. "I am." He remains where He's standing and just stares at me.

I say, "Okay, well ... You're not moving."

"The equipment is meant to carry two, not three." He sounds impatient.

I look at Him as if He's grown another head. "What are you *talking* about?"

He points to my alter ego, Theb, whose midsection I just grasped tightly with my arms in preparation for the descent. She stands fully erect and protectively in front of me. Though we are identical down to the last mole, my constant companion has perfect hair and a flawless complexion. And, unlike me, she isn't sweating in nervous anticipation. (Which is one of the many reasons I love her so much.)

"Who? *Her?* " I shake my head in confusion. "This is Theb! She's not a different person—she's me." Theb looks at the Lord, smiles sweetly, then nods her agreement. "Wherever I go, she goes."

He raises one eyebrow. "You need to leave her behind."

I snort with amusement. "What a laugh! That's impossible! What's next? You're going to tell me I have to have a kidney removed?" I squeeze Theb even tighter. She pats my hand approvingly.

He smiles. "Ah ... I do enjoy that sound—you laughing I

mean." The smile fades from His face slowly. "But I'm not kidding." Jesus' eyebrows pull together with sympathy but He looks straight at me, unwavering and resolute. "She cannot come with us."

Theb frees herself from my grasp and steps to my side. She folds her arms across her chest and furrows her brows as her gaze turns apprehensive.

I shake my head. "I don't understand. How can I go if she doesn't?"

Theb chimes in with a hurt tone. "Yeah, we're sort of a *package* deal."

"Two words," Jesus says. "Paradigm shift."

I frown in confusion. "Para-what?"

Jesus gives a half-grin in response to the look on my face. "Paradigm. Paradigms *typically* reference the way a community views reality. But in this case, I'm talking about the individual—you, and the set of values and practices at work in your heart."

"O ... *kay* ... So You're saying that what I think, feel, and do is fueled by some sort of ... internal paradigm?"

"Yes. That's it exactly!" Jesus says.

"Well what in the world does that have to do with Theb?"

"At present, she's the one you've been giving credence to."

My hands fly up defensively. "Whoa, hold on! You think *Theb* is a paradigm?!"

He nods. "Yes, and a terrible one at that. She is your self-centeredness, your sin nature."

Theb sputters, "Hey! How dare you talk smack about me!

Who do you think you are?"

Jesus spears Theb with a look. "Truth."

"Ugh," Theb says as she rolls her eyes. "Spare me."

"Not gonna happen," He replies.

Theb throws down her hands in agitation. "That's not what I meant!"

"Okay." He pauses. "If you're not Beth's selfishness, then what *are* you?"

She looks at Him warily then opens her mouth to speak. "I'm not a *what,*" she enunciates, "I'm a *who.* And I happen to be Beth's oldest and dearest friend."

"So ... being the great friend you are, if I told you that Beth was being hurt *because* of you, would you agree to stay behind?" He arches both eyebrows. "For her benefit?"

Her eyes narrow to slits. "That could never be true. Therefore it's an invalid question." She speaks slowly and succinctly.

Jesus turns to face me; imploring me to understand. "Do you see yet? She's too frightened of losing her grip on you to even answer my question. It's not you she cares about. Self preservation is her *only* priority."

I scrunch my face. "But she can't be *all* bad—right? We've been together for so long ..." I trail off.

His eyes fill with pity. "I know. You love her. And thinking about not having her with you seems worse than cutting your own arms off. But you'll never become the woman I want you to be if you continue to follow *her.*"

I say nothing and eye Him warily.

"Following her was never part of the plan. You were

taught 'to put off your old self, which belongs to your former manner of life and is corrupt through deceitful desires, and to be renewed in the spirit of your minds, and to put on the new self, created after the likeness of God in true righteousness and holiness.'[11] She's your old self and she needs to—"

Theb cuts Him off with an agitated tone. "Don't listen to Him! He's lying!" She puts one hand on her hip and uses the other to jab defensively toward her chest. "I'm not the bad guy here!" She looks Jesus up and down and disgust creeps into her voice. "He *obviously* doesn't like me. He—" Her mouth turns down into a scowl. "He's simply a thug bent on trapping you under his oppressive thumb." She turns and points a finger at Him. "Liar, li—"

"Knock it off, Theb!" I say through clenched teeth. For the first time ever, the sound of Theb's voice is grating to my ears, making thinking impossible.

Theb's mouth snaps shut as her face turns a mottled shade of red. For a moment, she looks like she might cry, but instead snarls menacingly at me. I wince at the hostility then slowly turn back to Jesus.

"What were You saying?"

"For at one time you were darkness, but now you are light in the Lord. Walk as children of light (for the fruit of light is found in all that is good and right and true), and try to discern what is pleasing to the Lord."[12]

I wait for Him to say more and frown when nothing is forthcoming. "So," I say haltingly, "what is it that would please *You*?"

He gives me a half smile. "Stop fighting against the

paradigm shift. The minute you accepted what I did on the cross to pay for your sins and selfishness, you were given a new paradigm." He answers my question before I can even voice it. "Therefore, if anyone is in Christ, he is a new creation. The old has passed away; behold, the new has come.[13] Your new paradigm is the Holy Spirit. He needs to be the one calling the shots in your life instead of Theb."

Understanding spreads through me. "The Holy Spirit," I mumble. "I've heard of Him." I look at Jesus questioningly. "The Bible says His presence is a gift to every one of Your believers—right?"

A deep and somehow familiar voice behind me says, "Yep."

I gasp and whirl around. I know without being told it's the Holy Spirit. I study Him for long moments. The only word that springs to my mind is "power"—it seems to radiate off His solid frame.

Gaining my voice I say, "Well why haven't I ... I mean ... Wh—" My shoulders droop and I sigh in defeat. "Okay, what's wrong with me?" I pause, then say, "You've been with me ever since I asked Christ into my heart, haven't You?" My question comes out as more of a statement.

"Yes. Since you were seven." The Holy Spirit moves to stand before me and rests His strong hands on my shoulders. He waits to speak until my eyes finally meet His.

"While you've heard My voice before, You weren't able to see Me because Theb kept getting in the way. And the more you obeyed her, the less you could even hear Me." He pauses. "I spoke, but she clapped her hands over your ears." He glances in her direction. "Now that you've shut her up," He smiles slightly, "you can actually see Me. And hear My voice again." His hands return to His sides.

"But why?" I ask. "Why doesn't she want me to hear You?"

"For the desires of the flesh are against the Spirit, and the desires of the Spirit are against the flesh, for these are opposed to each other, to keep you from doing the things you want to do."[14] The Holy Spirit frowns. "Theb and I are at odds with each other—we have no common basis, measure, or standard of comparison. Ours is not, nor ever will be, a peaceful co-existence because we *both* require dominance. We both desire full control of your heart."

"Oh." Then I pause. "I guess that explains why You don't want her to tag along." Long moments pass in silence as I brood over the scenario. "But what will happen to her?"

I look over at Theb, then recoil as soon as my eyes take in her new form. Her once-supple skin now appears to be rotting. Her eyes are bloodshot and crazed; her body now strangely mangled.

The breeze on the precipice shifts, and I am assailed by the most atrocious smell I've ever encountered. My stomach spasms. With blinding speed, the Holy Spirit leans over me and sweeps my hair to the side just before I throw up. After a moment, I straighten shakily, a hand covering my nose and mouth.

"What. Is. That?"

The Holy Spirit answers, "Theb."

"What happened to her?"

He hands me a cloth to wipe my mouth. "Actually nothing. That's how she's always looked."

I look at Him incredulously. "Not to me!"

"Theb's specialty is pretense—she's whispered lies to you for years. She led you to believe you were naturally good and that *she* somehow managed to produce this goodness within you. Now the veil of deception has been ripped away and you're *finally* seeing her in her actual state. You're realizing you are not good on your own. The truth is, every one of your good thoughts and deeds are tainted."

Seeing He has my undivided attention, He says, "None is righteous, no, not one; no one understands; no one seeks for God. All have turned aside; together they have become worthless; no one does good, not even one. Their throat is an open grave; they use their tongues to deceive. The venom of asps is under their lips. Their mouth is full of curses and bitterness. Their feet are swift to shed blood; in their paths are ruin and misery, and the way of peace they have not known. There is no fear of God before their eyes."[15]

I swallow past a dry throat. "Wow," I say. "It really sucks to learn these things about myself." I give an arid little laugh.

"Well sure it would—" The Holy Spirit says. "—*if* that were the end of it."

I cock my head to the side. "All right ... I'm listening."

Jesus had been standing silent, intent on the exchange between me and the Holy Spirit. But He captures my attention again when He smiles so brilliantly it causes my breath to catch.

"You remember Paul from the Bible?"

"The one who wrote like half the New Testament?" I ask.

He nods. "Well he wrote something you need to hear. 'And we all, with unveiled face, beholding the glory of the Lord, are being transformed into the same image from one degree of glory to another. For this comes from the Lord who is the Spirit.'"[16]

I hesitate. "I don't understand what You're trying to say."

Jesus' tone is tender. "I love you, but it's not because of anything your perceived goodness has done. I loved you, even back when the rotting, putrid Theb was the only paradigm to be found. In My love for you, I died on the cross to make a way for you to be Mine—to free you from Theb's death grasp. And My love for you rages on as you fight against Theb to give the Holy Spirit dominance in your life. By allowing Him to be in control, your goodness will become genuine because you are becoming more and more like Me."

I draw in a deep, shaky breath then release it in a loud gush. "I don't know what to say. I mean, if I were You ... looking down on *me* ... I would've thrown in the towel a *long* time ago. Theb would have broken my heart, ticked me off, then slaughtered any vestige of love that remained. She would have annoyed me to no end. How freakin' long can one person continue on in their selfishness?"

Jesus' eyes twinkle as His lips turn upward into a grin. "Then it's a good thing you're not Me, isn't it!" He wiggles both eyebrows at me playfully as a slow smile tugs at the corners of my mouth. "For my thoughts are not your thoughts, neither are your ways my ways, declares the LORD. For as the heavens are higher than the earth, so are my ways higher than your ways and my thoughts than your thoughts."[17]

I am unable to control the unexpected joy that's bubbling inside me. "You're unbelievable, You know that?" I sneak a peek at the Holy Spirit and find a grin on His face as well.

Jesus speaks after a few moments. "Well ... you need to get going."

I start like He dumped a bucket of ice water on my head. "Y—You're sending me alone?"

He is quick to reply. "Not in the least! I meant *you* in the plural sense." He says. "The Holy Spirit is going with you."

The Holy Spirit puts on similar gear to mine and shoulders the formidable-looking backpack Jesus recently set down.

"But make sure to stay close to His side." Jesus' voice cuts into my observation. "Theb will hound you the rest of the way."

"Oh!" I say. "That doesn't sound very reassuring. Why aren't You coming to help?"

"Now that you can clearly see the Holy Spirit and hear His voice, you have Me in the *exact* way you need Me."

I chew on my lip for a moment but quickly feel comforted. "Okay," I say.

It suddenly dawns on me I won't be as heavy without Theb to weigh me down. My delighted laugh echoes off the nearby boulders.

• Chapter 4 •
Lassie, Timmy's Fallen Down a Well Again

There's some illogical part of me that still believes if you want Superman to show up, first there's got to be someone worth saving.

My Sister's Keeper, Jodi Picoult[1]

I'd like to be a hero just so I could have my own theme music. The tune would be a mixture of hip hop, jazz, and funk swirled together in a ballad so hauntingly optimistic, people in distress would hear it and laugh in the face of their evil tormentors. My self-appointed theme music is an actual song called *Ikes Mood I* by Visioneers (in case anyone is wondering).

Alas, I'm no hero. If anything, I've actually gravitated toward the opposite end of the spectrum. No, not the villain.

The person in need of rescue.

You know, the princess in the tower guarded by fire-breathing dragons.

I wrote my own princess-in-distress story in the fourth grade. My brief narrative—bound in pink construction paper—was about a royal adolescent who found herself stranded on a desert island and was subsequently rescued by the love of her life.

I admit the plot was a bit lackluster. There were no dragons. No villains. The bulk of the story depicted the princess sipping on coconut water and giving exotic spa treatments to her adopted parakeet while waiting on her dashing swashbuckler. Of course, in the end, the princess and her man were married and lived happily ever after.

Even though it was not apparent to me at the time of my story's creation, I've come to realize I have always fantasized about being rescued. I've romanticized it, idealized it, and set it up on a lofty pedestal as the coolest thing that could ever happen to me.

Why?

Because a person is only rescued if they are important to the rescuer. And I am a narcissist-in-recovery, so it doesn't take a genius to figure out I enjoy being important to people.

But surely that's not the only component to rescue. The word itself has confinement, violence, danger, and/or evil mixed into its definition. Those words denote pain, fear, and suffering. That doesn't quite match the pretty picture I've painted in my mind of me waiting on a pristine beach with gentle island creatures bringing me food and making my shelter while I anxiously await my hero's helicopter. Not even close. Obviously, one is not rescued because they are having the time of their life on an accidental island getaway.

I cannot think about rescue without also taking note of villains. That isn't to say the only form of rescue is when a person is saved from a bad guy. I know natural disasters and accidents also happen. But this chapter is not a rerun of Lassie saving Timmy from yet another hazardous and unsupervised well.

Even as an adult, there is one fictitious villain I can't muster the courage to scrutinize. Seriously. I just Googled this monster and had to squint my eyes while I scrolled past the pictures that popped up at the top of my search. And even the *squinty* view of Pennywise the Clown from the movie *It* makes me want to vomit, pee my pants, and cry at the same time.

I've had issues from the moment I saw his tufts of red hair and evil-clown smirk gracing the cover of the November 1990 issue of TV Guide. A friend in elementary school felt compelled to narrate scenes from the movie before I could manage to silence her: Pennywise reaching out from a photograph, Pennywise hiding under beds, Pennywise coming out of a water faucet. That night at home, I felt his TV Guide eyes following me as I crossed the living room. It was all I could do—careful to touch as little of the publication as possible—to flip it facedown. But I knew he was still there. Clowns and I have not been on speaking terms ever since.

There's another villain in my life that is, unfortunately, all too real. I Googled him as well, but the pictures were laughable. In them he is red, has horns, and his teeth are bad enough to rival Austin Powers. One of my favorite SNL sketches features Garth Brooks as himself and Will Ferrell as Satan. Garth sells his soul to the devil for a hit song idea, only Satan stinks as a songwriter.

If the Will Ferrell devil was the extent of what I had to worry about, I'd be okay. The worst danger I'd face is potentially laughing myself to death. But, alas, the devil is a real adversary often not taken seriously. My belief that this statement is true only serves to open up a hearty can of worms; burdensome questions for which I simply have no answer. If God is holy and without sin, where did the evil come from that Lucifer embraced, subsequently getting him kicked out of heaven? How does he have so much power? Why does God allow Satan to wreak havoc on the earth? I wish I could understand. *However,* not knowing why or how doesn't change the fact I have a powerful enemy who loathes me.

Loathes me?

What did I do to him?! Maybe it's not me specifically. I think he's just angry in general.

> Therefore, rejoice, O heavens and you who dwell in them! But woe to you, O earth and sea, for the devil has come down to you in great wrath, because he knows that his time is short!
>
> Revelation 12:12[2]

In the context of the verse, the word *woe* is used as an

exclamation of grief, distress, or lamentation. The writer of Revelation is saying more than "it sucks to be you, earth." The author is saying that the earth is in serious danger. Humanity has a grave foe. He is called by many different names, but remains the same ancient villain.

> Now war arose in heaven, Michael and his angels fighting against the dragon. And the dragon and his angels fought back, but he was defeated, and there was no longer any place for them in heaven. And the great dragon was thrown down, that ancient serpent, who is called the devil and Satan, the deceiver of the whole world—he was thrown down to the earth, and his angels were thrown down with him.
>
> Revelation 12:7-9[3]

So what happens if the very people in need of rescue are not *aware* that they need it? What if the danger is unrecognizable? Shakespeare said in *King Lear*, "the prince of darkness is a gentleman."[4] The devil may be a lot of things, but he is no fool. He does not present himself to the human race as the bad guy. "... Even Satan disguises himself as an angel of light."[5] He's a master at subterfuge.

Allow me to make a comparison. I'll pretend I am a freshwater minnow. I'm going with the flow, minding my own fishy business and looking for my next meal. I finally spot a big fat worm writhing to and fro in the current. It is so beautiful. My mouth waters (or maybe it goes dry instead). It is the most luscious morsel of nematode I've ever laid my beady eyes on. I look around and realize no one else has noticed my prize.

I glide in for the kill, mentally savoring my food. BAM! Before I realize what's going on, my scales are sliced in two by the powerful jaws of an alligator snapping turtle that just consumed *me* for dinner. What I thought was my next delectable dining experience was actually the turtle's tongue disguised as a worm. And I fell for it.

The devil acts very much like the snapping turtle. He is as patient as he is deceptive. This is easy to understand considering he's the quintessential predator. He fights dirty. Below the belt is the only place he aims. He is so good he has some people convinced the prison in which he's entrapped them is far better than what is outside. They're aware of their captivity, but it's what they've always known. So they fear anything else.

> He was a murderer from the beginning, and does not stand in the truth, because there is no truth in him. When he lies, he speaks out of his own character, for he is a liar and the father of lies.
>
> John 8:44b[6]

Is it so difficult to believe that mankind would be duped by him?

• • •

The Holy Spirit and Jesus stand close by, talking quietly as I watch. Jesus puts His hand on the Holy Spirit's backpack-laden shoulder.

"Walk Me back down the path a bit before you and Beth head out."

The Holy Spirit nods, then looks at me and closes the gap between us in two long strides. His eyes are imploring.

"I need you to wait for Me."

My heart starts to pound unnaturally as I sense foreshadowing in His simple command.

"It is imperative for you to remain here until I return. Do you understand?"

I grasp at what He's *not* saying, but give up after a few moments.

"I do. I mean—" I laugh anxiously. "—how hard can it be to wait?"

A sad smile tugs at one corner of His mouth. He pulls me into a tight embrace and leans down to whisper in my ear.

"Don't forget who you belong to. I'm always with you even when you can't see or feel My presence." He gently squeezes me even tighter. "I love you," He adds. Then He releases me and straightens. "I shouldn't be too long."

He walks back, clasps Jesus' shoulder, and they walk purposefully away from me and the edge of the cliff. Their forms disappear beyond a cluster of spruce and cedars.

"O—kay." I say, though both are out of earshot.

I search for something to do. I start to walk toward the

edge of the cliff—to take a quick peek over—but wimp out within the first few steps. My lack of courage causes me to laugh at myself and sit with a boulder at my back instead. I let my head fall back and allow the gleaming sunlight to relax me as I drift off to sleep.

I awake with a start, disoriented. Pulse pounding in my ears, I glance around to see what roused me. Footsteps sound from the nearby grove. Calm floods my senses as I realize the Holy Spirit must be back.

But the figure that emerges into the light is not Him. It's not Jesus either. I wasn't expecting anyone else.

I observe the man walking toward me. He wears a pleasant expression on his handsome face. Well, actually, handsome isn't an adequate description. Breathtakingly beautiful is more like it. He is the sum of every dashing actor and male supermodel I've ever seen.

I feel my hands go clammy and fear I might be blushing. I scramble to my feet but keep my back plastered to the boulder for support. He finally walks close enough for me to feel the warmth in his gaze.

He offers me his hand. "Hi," he says brightly. "I'm Neyem."

I extend my sweaty palm and he takes it, pumping it up and down in his firm grasp. I decide his voice is positively enchanting.

I say the first thing that comes to my jittery mind. "That's an—uh—unusual name." My eyes slide shut as I mentally kick myself for sounding so lame.

His rich laugh holds no hint of mockery.

"Yes, it certainly is. It means *beautiful one*."

Of course his name would mean that! I blush again, detecting a mental wink aimed in my direction. I determine to keep my mouth shut.

"So," he starts conversationally. "You're waiting on the Holy Spirit?"

I nod. "You know Him?"

He smiles at me reassuringly. "Oh yeah. We're old friends," he exclaims. "We go back a *long* way."

"That's cool." Awkward silence. "So ... what are you doing up here?"

"The Holy Spirit didn't tell you?" Neyem looks puzzled. "I'm going with you guys. He asked me to keep you company until He gets back."

"Oh," I manage, wondering how long it will take for me to stop being flustered in his company.

"I told Him I wouldn't dare refuse being in the presence of such a charming beauty like yourself." This time his wink is not mental.

If I flush one more time, I'm sure my face will burn off. I mumble a shy, "Thank you."

Neyem takes my hand, kisses it gallantly, then leads me over to a comfortable-looking patch of underbrush to sit down.

"So," he starts off, "what shall we talk about while we wait? Politics?" He shakes his head. "No—that's too dreary. Fashion?" He pauses. "Not interesting enough."

His lips curl upward in a smile and he cocks his head to one side as he looks me square in the eye. "What I'm *really* interested to hear about is you. Tell me everything about you."

His presence fills my mind and nearly overwhelms me. I bite my lower lip and look down.

"Well—there's not that much to me. I'm a plain Jane."

Neyem laughs softly.

"You are many things, but plain is not among them. You're mysterious and beguiling. Tell me what you want out of life. What are your desires?"

I shiver, then swallow hard.

"I guess I want to have a good story." My statement comes out as more of a question. "I want to matter. And I—" my voice falters "—I want to feel whole."

"Beautiful," he murmurs. "You deserve all those things and more. Much, much more." With the last statement, his eyes fill with an unspoken promise.

"I do?"

"Unequivocally. That's one of the reasons I was asked to come along."

I raise one eyebrow in unspoken question.

"The Holy Spirit and I will sort of play tag team. He'll fill the role of your guide. And I'm the one with the power. I'll give you what you need ... and what you want," he says smoothly.

"Oh." I blink. His confidence slams the door on my questions.

"In fact, we should probably get going."

"But the Holy Spirit's not back yet," I say in protest.

"I know." He looks down at his wrist to examine an

extravagantly complicated-looking watch.

"The Holy Spirit told me if He wasn't back by now to start down the trail and He would catch up with us." Looking up and catching my unspoken concern, he smiles sardonically.

"The Holy Spirit's guide skills aren't necessary yet—I'm familiar with the trail."

Something about his statement bothers me.

"Trail?" I say, confused. "The gear the Holy Spirit and I have on made me think we're rappelling, not hiking." I point to him. "And you don't have *any* gear."

His voice is reassuring.

"We are rappelling. We have to take a trail to get to our starting point and my gear is already there. There's no way we can begin from up here—it is entirely too dangerous."

Hearing the phrase "dangerous" makes my forehead wrinkle with concern; but I feel a bit foggy and cannot, for the life of me, remember why the word triggers my hesitation.

"Look," Neyem says gently. "I know you're having a hard time accepting what I'm saying. But the Holy Spirit really did send me on ahead. He and Jesus were taking longer than they anticipated. He doesn't want you to be on the trail at night. And it doesn't make sense to wait around for Him since we've got so much ground to cover. He'll catch up quite easily—I assure you."

The more he talks, the more my mind turns to mush. I know the Holy Spirit told me to wait, but Neyem's points feel valid. *The two of them are old friends—why would he lie to me? Maybe it's just his extraordinary presence I'm having difficulty adjusting to.*

Neyem's magnetic eyes search mine expectantly.

He stands, then lowers one hand to help me up. "You ready?"

"I guess," I say as I accept his offered hand.

Neyem gives me a smile that causes my heart to stutter, then—still holding my hand—leads me in the opposite direction of the grove of trees the Holy Spirit disappeared through. After walking a few yards I make out a wide, rocky path in front of us.

We begin our journey in a comfortable silence, but he is soon pointing out small things of interest. He chatters on easily and I find myself laughing at his bold, outlandish statements. I grow comfortable in his presence and lose my speaking inhibitions. He asks me questions and, as I prattle on with great detail in my answers, I discover him to be an excellent listener.

The trail becomes increasingly rocky and steep. I realize we are moving upward. The air feels cooler even though I feel a trickle of sweat run down my back. Neyem turns often to help me over treacherous places, sometimes even lifting me in his strong arms when necessary. Each time he puts me down, he touches my cheek or chin in apparent adoration, sending chills down my spine.

The path makes a sharp turn to the right and I gasp as a dazzling house built into the mountainside comes into view.

"Welcome to my humble abode," Neyem says with obvious pride in his voice.

My eyes bulge in astonishment. *"You live here?"* No

wonder he didn't need help with this part of the trail.

"Yep." His grin is huge. "It makes for a great stopping place for lunch, does it not?"

My stomach answers with a resounding growl before I can even open my mouth.

"Heck yes it does!" I say.

Neyem deftly leads me around to the front door and lets us both inside.

"The bathroom is that way." He points down a wide hallway to the door at the end. "I'll get started on some food."

Once inside the bathroom, I marvel at the sections of the house I have seen—entire walls in warm shades of glass tiles, mahogany flooring, vivid and framed canvas landscapes. Even the bathroom boasts with its bronzed fixtures, huge marble tub, and the softest towels I've touched in my life.

Upon my return to the hallway, I follow the scent of melting butter and find Neyem busy in the kitchen. I don't ask how he knew to make grilled cheese sandwiches or why I see more of my all-time favorite foods scattered on the granite counter tops.

"Dang, this stuff looks incredible! Why are you tormenting me with all the foods I can't have? I'm really trying to watch my calories."

He laughs good-naturedly.

"Don't you remember me telling you that I'm the one with the power? The one who would give you not only what you need, but what you want as well? I hate to sound like the latest diet trend but, if you stick with me, you can eat what you love and actually lose weight while doing it!"

My eyes bulge. "What are you—my fairy godmother?"

He laughs again. "Nope. No wings," he says with a wink. "I just want you to get what you deserve—happiness."

He slides a heaping plate to me. One bite tells me it is the most amazing food I've ever experienced.

As I'm savoring a bite of my buttery grilled cheese sandwich, he says, "Come on. Let me give you the tour."

I carry my half-eaten sandwich as he walks me through room after room of stunning mountain views and opulent decor. I stop dead in my tracks when we reach his entertainment room. The tall wall is covered in movie titles, which I walk over to and examine. Everywhere I look, I see another one of my favorite romances.

"Would you like to watch one?" he asks. "While you finish eating, I mean?"

"I would love to. I think I could use a little break!"

Neyem turns on the gigantic TV and starts a movie. He lowers the lights and exits the room.

As soon as I sink onto the plush couch and the opening credits roll, I am transfixed. Not quite satisfied when it's over, I re-watch all my favorite parts again. Feeling no sense of urgency to leave the room and get started down the trail, I look through the film titles once more. Surely I have time for another.

I put on a new flick. Neyem must have brought in more goodies while I wasn't paying attention, because my plate is again piled high.

"This is the life," I murmur to myself as I settle in with the richest brownies I've ever eaten. I distractedly note a vague haze coiling around me, but I brush it off as nothing.

By the time I emerge from the darkened movie room, I notice the fading sunlight streaming through a window. Seeing that the day is drawing to a close makes me realize I forgot all about the Holy Spirit. I panic and search frantically for Neyem.

I find him casually flipping through a magazine in the main living room. He glances up when I race in.

"Enjoy yourself?" he asks.

"Yes," I say, breathless from my mad dash through the mini-palace. "Is He here yet?" I blurt out.

"Actually, I was coming soon to tell you not to worry. While you were relaxing, He contacted me to let me know He probably wouldn't get here until the morning." He pauses. "I'm sure you're tired. Would you like to camp out in one of the guest rooms? I guarantee you'll sleep better here than you would have out there on the cold, hard path."

My shoulders sag with a mixture of relief and gratitude. "Sure. Thanks."

Neyem leads the way up a massive, curving hardwood staircase. The door he opens at the top of the landing makes me gasp in wonder. Out of the corner of my eye, I see his smile at my response.

"I can tell you like it," he says. "Make yourself at home and let me know if you need anything. I'll see you in the morning." He tweaks my chin and heads back down the stairs.

I close the door and lean back against it, looking around. The bed is huge yet inviting. The room is covered in soft gray and muted gold. I can see into the full, private bath and realize its sleek lines and high-end fixtures could very well secure the house a spot on an HGTV show. Opposite the bed is a soft-looking, leather couch facing a smaller version of the entertainment den I recently vacated.

I step fully into the room and look back at the wall on which I just rested. The shelves lining it are crammed full of books. The titles I can make out are the very ones I've always wanted to read. Other than needing food, I feel certain I will never wish to leave this room.

I grab one of the books and flop onto the bed. My eyes devour the printed words until they become heavy and I fall into a deep slumber.

I awake only because of the grumbling of my stomach. When I walk downstairs, I find out the Holy Spirit is further delayed. My disappointment is quelled as I eat my astounding breakfast. True to Neyem's word, I feel my unwanted weight sloughing off with each new bite. I return to my room with Neyem's urging to relax while I wait.

This launches an emergent pattern. I fall prey to a fantasy world of good stories. I am unaware of time passing; days and nights become a blur. I can no longer tell the difference between reality and fantasy. There is only my demand for constant entertainment; my need for newer and better stories, movies, and foods.

Over time, I stop inquiring about the Holy Spirit's appearance.

One night, I awake in a fearful haze. Heaviness presses on me; my limbs are heavy as lead. My heart is shriveled and cold. Bleak. I feel the dim awareness of isolation. A tear squeezes out of the corner of my eye and drops onto the pillow.

"Help. Please," I manage in a dry whisper, though I'm not aware of whom I am asking it. Exhausted, I roll over and fall back into a fitful sleep.

When my eyes blink open again, an eerie glow pierces an even gloomier darkness. I sit up with a jolt of surprise and feel hard rock beneath my hands instead of the soft comfort of the mattress.

"What?" I attempt to rub the stiffness out of my shoulders. "Where am I? How did I get here?"

I glance around the dim surroundings and realize I'm in a cave of some sort. It is dank and cold. As I slowly get to my feet, pain shoots through my body with every joint I unlock. I bump something with my foot.

Looking down to my feet, I see a dish filled with some sort of disgusting, worm-riddled slop. I gag and kick the offensive bowl away.

"Oh—you're awake!" Neyem's voice sounds a moment before he steps out from a darkened tunnel on the opposite side of the cave.

"Where are we?" I call out in confusion.

"Well, I suppose it was only a matter of time before you figured it out." As he walks closer I notice a cold expression on his gorgeous face. "We're in the same place we've been all along."

The hair on the back of my neck pricks up. "Wh—what do you mean?" I stammer, unable to process the change in his demeanor or what he's saying.

"I mean the entire time we've been at 'my house' we've been in this cave. Only—you saw everything as I wanted you to see it. So," he drawls. "What do you think of your new home?" His smile is malicious.

I shake my head in disbelief. "I don't understand."

Neyem's only response is a long and cruel laugh that makes me blanch.

"What's the meaning of this?"

"You really want to know why?" he asks. His feet crunch on the loose stones as he paces, pausing for effect. "I hate you." He spits out. "I loathe your existence. You are such a stupid, pathetic creature!"

"But you—"

His snicker cuts me off and fills me with dread.

"Yes, I completely fooled you didn't I? You thought I was your friend," he jeers. "You thought I cared about you. You—" He suddenly doubles over with laughter. "You actually *believed* that slop you were eating was amazing food and that it would make you slimmer!"

I look at the discarded dish near my feet with horror. My eyes swing down to my middle and I observe my bulging waistline.

"Oh," he muses, "This is the most fun I've had in a while! Only, I hate that I didn't get to see the look on His face when *He* realized you came with me."

I know instinctively the "He" Neyem references is the Holy Spirit.

"What are you going to do with me?" I whisper in fear.

"Make you pay," he says swiftly. "For His treachery. But don't worry," he adds with perceptible glee. "I plan on having lots of fun at your expense!"

The horror of the situation wraps its fingers around my throat, causing me to gasp faster and faster until I'm hyperventilating.

I am being held captive by a madman. Not good. Not good. Trembling, my eyes rove my prison, hoping for any method of escape. They find nothing because I see no way past my jailer.

I lean back against the cold rock and force myself not to panic. I cannot stem the flow of hot tears that fall to the rock floor. *Not good. Not good.*

Think. I clench and unclench my hands. If only I could let the Holy Spirit know where I'm at. Maybe He would come for me.

Suddenly I remember the iPhone that was once in my pocket. I carefully slide my hand into my pocket and feel the phone resting against my leg where I last left it. If I can just get a moment without Neyem hovering over me, maybe I can send out a message. I grasp the device in my pocket for the lifeline it is.

"Have you figured out yet there's no escaping me?"

I start violently as Neyem's voice breaks through my thoughts of escape. My hand jerks out of my pocket and I watch in dismay as the phone I was gripping flies through the air and lands several feet away.

Before I can even blink, Neyem snatches it up.

"Oh that's just precious! Thought you could place a call

for help?" He fiddles with it a few moments and hands it back to me, a sick grin on his face.

I look at the screen and discover there are zero bars in the infernal cave. His grin fades slowly and the eyes regarding me turn black. Fear claws at my throat.

"Things would've gone so much better for you if you'd never said yes to Him."

He traces my cheekbone with the back of one finger, as if caressing a trapped mouse sentenced to extermination. "I would've at least left you alone."

I jerk my face away from his touch.

"Who are you?" I croak.

His sentence forms a crisp staccato as he rolls his eyes. "I am ... irritated ... that you even have to ask." He walks around me slowly and stops at my back. He leans in, lips grazing my ear, and whispers, "Let's just say you made a *huge* mistake when you chose what team you wanted to play for."

Before I realize what he's doing, his arm darts around my neck and squeezes, cutting off my air supply. My hands flail behind me and grasp for a way to gouge his eyes and stop his attack. But he is entirely too quick and powerful. I hear his amused laughter through the roar in my ears.

Just as I am about to succumb to blackness, he releases his grip and I collapse on the floor, gasping mouthful after mouthful of stale air.

"Are you going to kill me?" I whisper hoarsely.

"Now why would I want to waste my toy?" I sink my forehead slowly to the cool stone below. Neyem starts talking again, but I'm too lost in misery to notice what he's saying.

I wish I had never met him. I wish I never believed him; I'd still be in the clearing waiting on the Holy Spirit. Why didn't I wait? I wish the Holy Spirit was here to help me.

As soon as the thought forms, my head snaps up as I hear the voice of the One I long for. It's faint. But it is undoubtedly the Holy Spirit.

"Beth! Don't believe Neyem. You're mine—*always*! I promised."

"Where are You?" The desperate cry burns my tender throat.

Neyem believes the question is aimed at him. "Right here," he replies with heavy sarcasm. "Obviously."

The Holy Spirit's voice is a little louder. "I am with you. You're going to have to listen very carefully to Me. Say only what I tell you to."

I nod, even though I'm not sure He can actually see me. Neyem launches a snarling tirade and I clasp my hands over my ears to drown him out. This enrages him.

"Listen to me!" he screams. He hauls me up to my feet and pins my wrists behind my back. I struggle against him to no avail.

Amazingly, I hear the Holy Spirit's voice more clearly, even though Neyem's rants are growing hysterical. I still. I listen to His instruction and then dip my head slightly in acknowledgment.

My mouth opens and I whisper, "Neyem, you have no power over me. I belong to God, who bought and paid for me through Jesus Christ's blood. He alone has the victory, not you."

Neyem grunts, then releases his grip on me like I burned him.

I dart over to the opposite side of the cave. He stares down at his hands with an inscrutable look on his arrogant face. Then his eyes lock with mine and they narrow.

He knows about the Holy Spirit!

He slides toward me slowly.

Suddenly, the gritty sound of horns and an electric guitar signaling the beginning of *Ike's Mood I* fills the cave. My jaw barely has time to drop in awe before a massive quake showers rocks all around us. I throw my arms up for protection, but there is no need. The tumult only lasts thirty seconds and I am unscathed. I still hear my Hero's theme music playing as I lift my head to see a large opening in the cave directly across from me.

Warm daylight rushes in and the Holy Spirit fills the space; dust and dirt swirl around His massive frame just as the female singers begin to croon in *Ikes Mood I.* The Holy Spirit rushes in, grabs Neyem by the neck, and drags him like a rag doll outside.

"Don't touch her," roars the Holy Spirit above the music.

"She's nobody," Neyem counters with a hate-filled voice. "Nothing more than a stupid piece of trash—"

The Holy Spirit's impassioned growl cuts off Neyem's accusations against me. I hear what sounds like fist meeting flesh as the Holy Spirit unleashes His fury on Neyem. Between each volley, Neyem screams obscenities directed at me and his attacker.

From my vantage point, I see the Holy Spirit finally

throw Neyem to the ground in disgust. The monster limps away faster than I would've thought he could—based on the comprehensive beat-down he just received—and is quickly out of sight.

As the song trails to an end, the Holy Spirit surges into the cave and gently picks me up. He walks back out into the sunlight and sits on the ground, His back to the wall of my former prison.

With great care, He settles me in His arms and tucks my head under His chin. The shaking catches me off guard and, in the span of a moment, my body is overrun by tremors. A giant tear pools in my eye then drips onto my cheek. It follows the curves of my face until it has no other option but to splatter on the collar of my shirt. Sobbing follows.

The Holy Spirit kisses the top of my head and then rests His cheek against the same spot. He covers my face with a giant hand and begins to rock back and forth, soothing me.

"You're safe," He whispers over and over.

Only when my own trembling subsides do I realize the Holy Spirit is crying too. I feel His muscles tense with each sob that racks His body. He finally takes a deep, ragged breath and lifts His head.

"Thank You," I say, when I'm able to speak again.

He gives me a soft squeeze, and then gets to His feet, still holding me in His arms.

"You're welcome." His eyes are red and puffy and hold a slightly haunted look. He notices me studying Him and gives me a small smile.

"Let's get out of here." He starts back down the path

toward the clearing where He told me to wait, still carrying me.

I wrap my arms around His neck and lean my head on His chest. “I have so many questions I don't know where to start,” I say with a sigh.

“Well,” He begins softly, “First you need to recognize who that was. His name does *not* mean beautiful one.” He pauses. “His name means: *My* enemy.”

“*Your* enemy?”

“Yes. Mine.” He sighs. “He's no match for Me—not even close. So he tries to hurt Me the only way he can. Through you. He can't have your eternal soul; you've already given that to Me. *But,* the rest of you is fair game.”

My lips form a silent “oh.” I’m struck by a thought. “If he's no match for You, why can't You just destroy him and be done with it?”

His sigh is deeper now. “It's not time yet. His day of destruction is coming, I promise you that. But it's not today.” He tightens His hold on me. “That’s why I want you to keep your guard up. You must *always* be prepared for his attacks.”

“There will be more attacks?” I ask with dread.

I feel the Holy Spirit nod.

“They won't stop as long as you're alive. Unfortunately, there will be times in the future—” His voice cracks, “when he’ll catch you with your guard down. And he’ll succeed in trapping you again.”

“No!”

“Neyem’s cunning. He's the personification of evil. And you are human. Sometimes you’ll forget Me, ignore Me and, at times, even *want* to go with Neyem. But I'll fight for you. And come to your rescue. Always, and every time."

I whisper dejectedly, "But why bother?"

He whispers back, "Because you matter to Me." And then He carries me the rest of the way down the trail.

• Chapter 5 •
A Consuming Fire

"I haven't seen you like this before."

"Isn't it supposed to be like this?" He smiled. "The glory of first love, and all that. It's incredible, isn't it, the difference between reading about something, seeing it in the pictures, and experiencing it?"

Twilight, Stephenie Meyer[1]

Sometimes I'll go on YouTube and watch the music video for Eminem's *Love The Way You Lie.* And then I hit replay a few more times. I can't get enough of the video, but it's not because of Eminem's smooth lyrics (minus the f-bombs) or Rihanna's interesting black ensemble.

The video is *intense.*

Yes, I know it's about a dysfunctional relationship, but their intensity draws me in. I can't help myself. The couple, played by Megan Fox and Dominic Monaghan, ooze passion. They scream at each other, throw punches, break things, then make out; meanwhile, in the background, a house is in flames. The whole thing fascinates me.

I'm a big fan of intensity. I sort of revere it. How intensity is generated, I do not know. But when it's paired with love, a fierce duo is born. To observe the two in action takes my breath away.

This duo is my favorite component in a good love story because the characters become consumed by their feelings for each other. Time and space cease to exist. The only concrete thing in their universe is the object of each one's affection—the other. The couple's singular desire is to be together, whatever the cost. And, if death threatens to steal one party, the other would forfeit his or her own life in hopes of saving their beloved.

All that being said, I think it's fairly easy to see why I'm such a *huge* fan of Edward and Bella's relationship in the *Twilight* series. Sure it starts out a bit ... twisted. Boy meets girl. Boy wants to *eat* girl. Boy goes against his intrinsic urges and instead falls in love with said girl. Intensity swiftly enters the picture. The following is a look at one of the first intense moments between the two:

> He lifted his glorious, agonized eyes to mine. "You are the most important thing to me now. The most important thing to me ever."
> My head was spinning at the rapid change in direction our conversation had taken. From the cheerful topic of my impending demise, we were suddenly declaring ourselves. He

> waited, and even though I looked down to study our hands between us, I knew his golden eyes were on me.
>
> "You already know how I feel, of course," I finally said. "I'm here ... which, roughly translated, means I would rather die than stay away from you."
>
> "... And so the lion fell in love with the lamb ..." he murmured. I looked away, hiding my eyes as I thrilled to the word.
>
> *Twilight,* Stephenie Meyer[2]

Sigh. I like intensity. But, oddly, I am repelled by it if it involves me ...

I met my husband during my first day of high school. August 1994. In Algebra I class. As soon as I found a desk by the window, a boy with dark hair and defined muscles made his way to a seat across the aisle. I thought he was cute but, then again, I'd hit high school and I thought *a lot* of guys were cute. He introduced himself as Jerimiah, and his engaging smile and sense of humor sealed our friendship before class came to an end.

In the weeks and numerous conversations to follow, I figured out that Jerimiah had developed a crush on me. I never minded being the object of a boy's admiration, so I tried to make it as easy as possible for him to like me. Our lunch tables were quite close to each other and I sat in the best position for him to watch me having the time of my life with my friends. I caught him smiling my way more than once.

But Jerimiah made a fatal mistake midway through my freshman year. He conned me. He claimed he couldn't make it all the way to his locker between lunch and Algebra, and wondered if he could store a few things in mine. Being an agreeable friend, I naively entrusted him with my combination and thought no more of it.

A few days later, I opened my locker and discovered some uninvited guests. The teddy bear was adorned in a frilly white ensemble, clutching a single red rose in one paw and an original poem in the other. For the sake of our future generations, I won't recite the poem.

Unfortunately for Jerimiah, he hadn't read my "Rules of The Chase" handbook. The book *clearly* stated it was important for the Chaser to play the role of the rebel-scum-scoundrel-Han-Solo. And Han would *never* have put a froufrou stuffed animal in Leia's locker. He would've swaggered up to her between classes—his body oozing rugged charm and Tommy cologne—and talked about, well, himself. There wasn't a sweet or attentive bone in Han's body.

I didn't mind Jerimiah liking me. I even flirted like crazy to help his crush along. I just didn't expect him to be upfront about how he felt, mainly because I didn't want to pin down my feelings for him.

Back at the crime scene, I slammed the metal door shut as quickly as possible—hoping no one passing by noticed the gaudiness within—and headed to Algebra. Plastering what I hoped was a serene look on my face, I walked to Jerimiah's desk, politely thanked him for the bear and poem, and slid into my assigned seat. Awk—ward. As my mind re-plays the moment, I hear a symphony of crickets.

Feeling the sting of my dismissal, he didn't speak to me much during the remainder of my freshman year. Can't say I blame him. He put his heart on the line and I politely shoved it away. Still, I couldn't quite convince myself to ditch the poem. Or the teddy bear.

By the time school released us for summer break, I had already gone through one figurative Han Solo. But I discovered real-life Han to be disappointing at best. He really *did* talk only about himself.

On a brighter note, Jerimiah and I ended up patching up our differences when we ran into each other that summer. I apologized for being a jerk and confessed to missing his friendship. He exonerated me and, *violá*, we were chummy once more.

There was only one problem. He had moved on from his Beth-crush and was dating someone else. My eyes shot green sparks. Only when I *couldn't* have him did I realize he was a cut above other guys. He was an unapologetic, non-dorky Christian who also happened to be witty and intelligent. It didn't hurt he had warm brown eyes and an understated, sexy cleft in his chin.

An entire year of our friendship passed before Jerimiah was again on the open market. I don't know if the locker scene haunted him or he simply knew me better by then. Either way, he didn't waste time telling me how he felt about me. He just asked me to do stuff with him, making the summer before my junior year and his senior one like something out of a young-love movie montage. We went fishing and rollerblading. We explored (some might call it trespassing) the hilly pastures near my house, covering them in cartwheels and laughter.

We were more than country bumpkins though. We hit the town. Jerimiah paid for my dinner at Golden Corral, which was about as fine dining as anyone could get in Inverness, Florida during the late '90's. Our hometown was fortunate enough to have a six screen movie theater so, while we witnessed Tom Cruise put his life on the line in *Mission Impossible,* Jerimiah *finally* got around to holding my hand.

During that part of our courtship, we did a *lot* of hand-holding. One could say our physical relationship did not progress as quickly as I thought it should. It took us eight months of dating before he kissed me for the first time. I was disheartened he hadn't made the attempt sooner. It's not like he was a vampire—he could kiss me without fear of being tempted to drain my body of its blood. So why wait?

Because of another woman.

Yes, I wrote that correctly. He was loath to tarnish the kissing experience with the woman he would *someday* marry. He even started a journal in high school to the future tramp. For her eyes only. He certainly hadn't identified her yet, but there he was holding out on smooching with *me*! Confession: I was, in fact, jealous of her, which is ironic because it turned out I was actually jealous of my future self. So I guess I take back the tramp part.

Just because he wrote to her/me didn't make him an

inattentive boyfriend. At school, he walked me to every class he could, often late to his own in order to accomplish this feat. He usually had a sweet note to encourage me. He prayed *for* and *with* me. I'm pretty sure that wasn't normal behavior for a pubescent boy.

He wasn't dating me to pass the time or because his sole motivation was to get in my Underoos. Jerimiah genuinely cared about who I would become as a person and seemed to want the best for me. He even joked about the possibly of a future together. I use the word 'joke' loosely, considering he informed my brother Joe during a game of Hearts he would someday marry me.

Judging from how much I longed for all things romantic, one would think my own chronicle would sweep me off my feet. Clearly, I liked Jerimiah. He was good to me. He was good *for* me. My family liked him; he was the only boy I ever brought home to my parents, and he *obviously* got along with my brother Joe. If my oldest brother Jon wasn't already away at college, I'm sure they would've done some grunting or other ritualistic male bonding too.

But I found myself squirming away from his sincere and wholesome affections. I wrote the following to God while Jerimiah and I were dating:

> *I don't know what to say to Jerimiah either. You know what was said today.* (Don't ask—no clue!) *Sometimes I get a little scared at the way he starts talking. I like being his good friend though. Please help me to*

> *straighten out my feelings and be completely honest with him.*

Not too long after the previously mentioned first kiss, Jerimiah and I made the mutual decision to stop dating. I was building a wall to distance myself and he could tell. Theoretically, I was drawn to his captivation with me. In reality, I felt smothered to the point of running and hiding out in a desert bunker. I commented to a friend that Jerimiah was the kind of guy I wanted to marry. I just didn't want to date him right then. I didn't want *anything* to do with his intensity toward me.

> "It's incredible, isn't it, the difference between reading about something, seeing it in the pictures, and experiencing it?"
>
> Edward Cullen[3]

Yes Edward. Yes it is. And Jerimiah wasn't the only one to experience my fear of intensity.

• • •

An azure sky is the sun's backdrop. The air is still, but teeming with life. The Holy Spirit carries me—without incident—back to the cliff where we'd started.

When we first break through the clearing, I scan the scenery with trepidation, expecting to see Neyem lurking. Feeling me stiffen, the Holy Spirit gives a gentle squeeze before setting me on my feet.

"It's good that you're wary," He says, "but Neyem and Theb aren't close by."

He walks over to a boulder near the edge. Sitting next to the stout granite is the formidable-looking backpack. I watch in awe as He shoulders it with ease.

"Wow. What's in there?"

"Our supplies," He says.

"Um," I say with reluctance, "Do You need me to help with any of that?" It sounds as ridiculous to say out loud as it did in my head.

"No, I think I've got this one." He smiles and winks at me. "You wouldn't be able to bear it even if you *really* wanted to."

I eye the pack and snort a laugh at my absurd offer of help. "You may be right."

His smile remains in place as He motions me over to the boulder. I notice the ropes tied around it and remember Jesus securing those same ropes what seems like ages ago.

The Holy Spirit reaches over and connects my harness to the ropes. Then He secures His own. Tugging firmly at both our straps, He makes the final safety check. Then He walks to the edge of the cliff and begins His instructions.

"You'll want to lean back over the edge like you're about to sit in a chair." He demonstrates. "Then, using your descender, you'll either walk down or push off the rock face. Gravity and the descender will swing you down a bit."

I cautiously lower myself on all fours to peer over the edge at Him. As I watch, He executes both maneuvers flawlessly. He comes to a halt and lifts His head in my direction.

"Think you got it?"

I stammer. "You—You're sure my equipment checks out … right? I just read about a guy who fell because his carabiner was faulty." My face contorts into a grimace.

When He doesn't answer, my eyes snap to His. His expression is calm.

"You can trust Me."

I nod, then reluctantly stand and back up to the edge. I have complete faith in Him but it doesn't stop the wild thrumming within my chest.

Duh-dum … duh-dum … duh-dum

To my chagrin, fearful tears leak down my flushed face. I don't bother to wipe them away.

I clumsily lean back over the nothingness and attempt to suppress the scream rising in my throat. My shaking feet take tiny, sliding steps down the uneven rock and I inch lower.

Disjointed. Clumsy.

To my surprise, it doesn't take me long, even at my snail's pace, to reach the Holy Spirit's position.

In a risky move, I angle my head to glance in His direction. He's staring at me and there's something in His eyes that captivates me and holds me still. I almost feel a quiet confidence begin to radiate through my tense muscles and nerves, making it possible to loosen my death-grip on the descender.

I am the first to break eye contact though.

His voice cuts through the silence. "So. It's not as bad as

you thought, is it?"

I still breathe delicately, as if that has some kind of control over my swaying. A small smile cracks my face as my eyes take in their new surroundings.

"It's really quite ... beautiful," I breathe. "Dizzying ... but beautiful."

"I know," He says with a proud smile.

Suddenly, He shimmies a few steps over, turns toward me and crushes me in a bear hug. I gasp in alarm and grab a hold of Him; clinging for dear life. I feel the rumble of laughter bubble up in His chest.

"Don't worry! I've got you."

He releases me after several moments of the most heartfelt embrace I've ever experienced, careful to make sure I'm not left swaying over the nothingness.

"What was that for?" I ask. I will my heart to slow.

He flashes me an exultant smile. "I'm pumped!"

I tilt my head, giving Him a quizzical grin in response. "Okay. Pumped about what?"

"You, of course!"

I look away, feeling shy.

"It's just that—" He cuts Himself off and starts over. "Well, do you have any idea how much I've looked forward to this day?"

I misunderstand His question. "But ... You're God. You can do anything You want. You can go rappelling any time! Heck, You don't even need this equipment! You could just ... float down."

I giggle as I get a mental picture of Him hovering by the

mountainside, sans equipment. In my vision, He's wearing perfectly-billowed Hammer pants. And because my mind is prone to tangents, I *almost* start to hum *Can't Touch This*.

"No, you goofy girl!" He says with a laugh and proceeds to ruffle my hair. "You said *yes* to Me."

"Oh!" Moments pass and I feel my cheeks grow warm. I squirm, disconcerted by His words. The longer He is silent, the more choked I feel. I become overwhelmed by the need to break the quiet and divert His attention.

"Right." I mumble awkwardly, hoping He will get the hint as I hesitantly move my gelatinous legs down the rock face.

He matches my pace and offers me a sympathetic smile. "I know what's going on in that mind of yours."

"Yeah?" I squeak.

"Mmm hmm. My intensity makes you uncomfortable. Always has." He pauses. "You like intensity in theory and even on paper, but not in reality."

My forehead wrinkles in confusion. "I'm not sure I follow You."

He pauses for a moment then replies, "You would much rather read about or watch an intense moment involving *other* people than to actually experience one yourself."

I chew on that for a stretch. Realizing He's right, I answer with a slight scowl. "*So what?*"

"Have you ever wondered why?" He asks.

I sound an annoyed *harrumph* before responding. "No. Why does it matter?"

"Wouldn't it be great to actually experience your own life instead of living vicariously through other people?" He asks.

Heat again floods my cheeks and I try to angle away from Him and His question.

"Come here," He says with a gentle voice. "I know you're irked. I promise I'm not making fun of you."

He stops to rest on a small outcropping of rock and there's just enough room for me to stand next to Him.

"You should at least try to think of the why."

I breathe a noisy sigh then give my bumbling response.

"I guess ... if I think someone is being intense toward me, I start to feel smothered." I shrug my shoulders slightly. "I can't seem to help it."

He turns to sit on the ledge, letting His legs dangle below. He motions for me to join Him and I gingerly position myself by His side.

"That's good. I want you to keep digging though. *Why* do you feel smothered?"

I chew on my lip as I think. I analyze for a long time before again opening my mouth to speak.

"What if I don't feel the same things back toward that person?" I say in a low voice.

He nods His agreement and flashes me a sad smile. "Yes," He says as He picks absentmindedly at the rock beneath Him. "That's one of the reasons you run from Me. You're uneasy because you don't love Me on the same level that I love you."

My face falls as I realize He's telling the truth. "Why can't I just love You in a ... a safe way? A *normal* way." I ask.

"Because I want more." He looks down at His hands. "In one regard, you're like Katniss was in *The Hunger Games*.

Though I'm not talking about your skills with a bow and arrow," He mumbles as an afterthought.

I furrow my eyebrows. "What?"

"Well in the book, Peeta loved Katniss. Had ever since they were kids. Yet, for the longest time, all she could do was fake affection for him."

"But they—"

"I know," He interrupts calmly. "They were under much different circumstances. And she did care for him. But how badly do you think it hurt Peeta every time he showed Katniss what was in his heart, knowing she didn't return his depth of feelings?"

"She did love him!" I argue in a gruff voice. "She just didn't know how much yet."

He continues as if I hadn't spoken. "Do you know how Peeta was able to do it? To love her so intensely?"

At His pause, I turn my head to look at the Holy Spirit's profile.

He says, "Peeta loved Katniss for Katniss. Not for the way she made him feel. Otherwise, his jealousy of Gale would've soured his love for her."

I look into the Holy Spirit's eyes. The agony I read in them makes my chest tighten painfully, and I know He's no longer thinking about Peeta and Katniss.

"What do you know of jealousy?" He asks, His voice rough with emotion. His strong jaw line is marred by the silent tears dripping onto His lap.

I blink. My thoughts drift to dark and unfounded fears of Jerimiah loving someone else. I can almost feel his powerful arms around me—I'm such a nice fit within their embrace. My blood turns to ice as I imagine those protective arms wrapped around another woman. I hate her, this faceless creature. I hate her for stealing away my love's gazes—the very ones that used to frighten me with their intensity.

"I've tasted it a few times," I say slowly.

"Well, you should know that I'm 'a consuming fire, a jealous God.'"[4]

"*You're* jealous?" I arch an eyebrow. "Of whom?"

"Anyone or anything stealing your love and affections away from Me."

Quiet falls. I fiddle with the hem of my shorts and do the only thing I can think of: imagine myself in His shoes. How would I feel if I loved someone so much that I died to save them, only to have them give me a polite "thank you" and then love me in word only? But that's not the worst of it. What if that person gave their heart away to everyone and everything *but* me—sorta like the Israelites back in the day. God delivered them time and time again, proving His love. But the nation of Israel prostituted herself to false gods. "She decked herself with her earrings and jewelry, and went after her lovers; but Me she forgot."[5] The phrase *"but Me she forgot"* seems to articulate God's heartache.

"I'm so sorry." I whisper raggedly. "I—" I swallow and start again. "I don't know how to not make You jealous."

He opens His mouth after several long moments. "Do you know when Katniss began to truly love Peeta?" He asks. I shake my head.

"When she was finally consumed by her thoughts for

him. It was as if everything inside her was connected to the singular thought of Peeta." He pauses for the span of a few heartbeats.

"That's what I want from you. I want you to be used up on Me. Spent. I want to hold your complete awareness—to consume you."

He reaches in His pack and pulls out a water bottle, offering it to me. I accept, and water dribbles down my chin in my haste to hydrate. I nod my thanks as I screw the cap back on.

"But what does that look like in real life?" I ask.

"One name—Josiah."

I raise both eyebrows expectantly and breathe out a soft laugh. "And?"

"He was one of the kings of Judah in ancient times."

"What was he like?" I ask.

"Well, unlike his predecessors, he walked in My ways. Eighteen years into his reign, he was read the Book of the Law, which was equivalent in his day to the Bible. When he heard the words and realized the extent of the people's disobedience to Me, he was distraught. I mean, he was beside himself, weeping and ripping his robe, which is what they did in his day as an outward expression of grief."

"So he was pretty torn up about it?"

He gives a sideways smile at my unintentional pun. "One could say that. Anyway, because he humbled himself before Me, Josiah was told he would not have to see the disaster I would bring upon his people. He would rule another thirteen years, then die, only having seen his kingdom experience peace."

"Ah," I say in a monotone voice. "Don't get me wrong, it seems You were generous. But the story feels a bit ... anticlimactic—"

His laughter cuts me off. "It would be, if Josiah's story stopped there."

"Oh?" I say.

"Do you think Josiah was content, knowing the rest of his days as king would be peaceful ones?" The Holy Spirit asks.

I shrug. "Probably. I mean, what else could he do? Disaster in the future was already promised, so why bother with the present?"

"My point *exactly.*" His tone is emphatic. "But bother with the present he did. Josiah gathered all the people of his kingdom together, from the least to the greatest, and read in their hearing all the words of the Book of the Covenant. Josiah and all the people renewed their covenant to follow Me. Then he destroyed all the temples and sacred articles that had been set up by his forefathers to worship fake gods. He got rid of every last little thing that separated the people from Me. One might even say Josiah was ... consumed with Me."

He stops talking. I fiddle with my water bottle.

"'Before him there was no king like him, who turned to the LORD with *all* his heart and with *all* his soul and with *all* his might ... nor did any like him arise after him.'[6] Jesus echoed those same words when He was asked what the most important thing is. 'You shall love the Lord your God with *all* your heart and with *all* your soul and with *all* your mind.'"[7]

He pauses. "Did you notice in each verse that the word *all* was reiterated three times?"

"It was kinda hard not to notice, with You emphasizing them so strongly." I tease.

He smiles. "Good. You're obviously smart enough to know what *all* means. But are you aware that when all is in adjective form, one of its definitions means all gone, consumed, spent?"[8]

I am unable to form a reply.

"Josiah may have been a king, but he was human. So, if he did it, you can too." His voice is soft. "Spend your heart on Me. Spend your soul on Me. Spend your mind on Me. Is what I'm asking for intense? You bet. But I want no less."

Before I can talk myself out of it, I take a deep breath, then reach out and clasp the Holy Spirit's hand. He gives a gentle squeeze and my hand is enveloped in His.

"I love You," I say, almost inaudibly.

"And I love you back."

He brings my hand up to His lips and kisses it. And this time, when He aims His huge smile at me, I don't look away.

• Chapter 6 •
When I Get Out Of the Joint

A man may leave prison, but he is still condemned.

Les Misérables, Victor Hugo[1]

There's a famous story I love, for a few reasons. It's a compelling tale of grace and transformation with a slice of romance à la carte. And the main character reminds me of myself in a few ways.

Les Misérables is the chronicle of escaped convict Jean Valjean, whose initial crime was stealing a loaf of bread to feed his starving family. He escaped prison several times, but was always caught and sentenced with additional punishment.

After nineteen years of hard labor and his release with a yellow ticket, he was an altogether different Valjean. He re-emerged into society as a free yet morally bankrupt creature. The yellow ticket he was forced to carry branded him "a very dangerous man."[2] Employers, in turn, paid him far less than a man doing the exact same job. He was turned away from every hope of lodging and food. (No one wanted a dangerous criminal under their roof, even if he was a paying customer.)

After everyone else (and I do mean *everyone*) refused him on the wintry evening of his release, he became the overnight guest of a poor bishop. This bishop did too many good things for me to list, so just believe me when I say he was a great man and helped people without prejudice. The bishop—Monseigneur Bienvenu—had nothing of value except "six silver knives and forks and a soup-ladle, and two large candlesticks of massive silver, which he had inherited from a great-aunt."[3] Of course Valjean-the-thief noticed the silver he was eating with at dinner. It was still on his mind when he woke in the middle of the night due to an "over-comfortable bed."[4] So it was no surprise he stole the valuable silverware and escaped the bishop's house under the cover of darkness.

I mentioned earlier that Jean Valjean reminded me of myself. While I've never been handcuffed or had to make license plates in prison, I am guilty of a crime. In the first chapter of this book, I said Jerimiah and I broke up briefly before getting engaged. Let me explain why.

Allow me to back up to the month before my high school graduation. This was long after the first time we broke up, and we were both on the open market. We remained good friends even after our breakup, so Jerimiah chillin at my house was not out of the ordinary.

On one such occasion, Jerimiah got sick of waiting for me to finish whatever it was I was doing, so he smeared a handful of Satinique shampoo (my parents were deep into Amway at the time) onto my dry tresses. I retaliated and we engaged in an epic shampoo battle. But hair care product wasn't the only thing flying. The sparks of attraction were palpable.

The next day, we met at a local park to discuss our relationship. While hanging on the monkey bars, we decided to become an official item—for the second time.

Those summer months leading up to my departure for college were good ones. They were filled with adolescent jobs, travel, and even talk of a possible future for the two of us. We were falling in love. It was the real deal. But college was on the horizon. And our schools were hundreds of miles apart.

Even though we knew long distance relationships were challenging, we both agreed to keep seeing each other exclusively.

Jerimiah braved an eight-hour car ride, the return half spent alone with my parents, in order to help move me into my dorm room. It was a tough goodbye, more so for him because, as nervous as I was, I was equally excited. I could be whoever I wanted to be at college. It was my opportunity for reinvention. I was starting out with new people who didn't know what I looked like before puberty and braces. The possibilities were endless: mysterious loner, bubbly blonde, witty intellectual. And though I had ample opportunity to be someone altogether new, old tendencies die hard: I was a pathological flirt.

If I could get into a time machine and have a little chat with my former self, I'd knock her out cold (strategically placing my KO blow, as to not mess up my post-braces smile). I know we all make mistakes and do things we regret, but what happened next took my proverbial cake.

Here's the low-down dirty-rotten secret: I cheated on Jerimiah during my first semester of college (yeah, I know—way to go the distance). What started out as simple flirting with another guy escalated into a clandestine relationship. With Jerimiah none the wiser.

I was a double agent. I got the love and security I craved from Jerimiah, and thrill and excitement from the other guy. However, I wasn't *completely* without feeling; guilt hammered me with a jab-hook combo each time I spoke to or saw Jerimiah. Toward the end of my first semester, my conscience won and I broke it off with the other guy.

Phew. I felt relieved. I'd finally done the right thing. And, though now carrying my own yellow ticket, I could forget my indiscretion and move on to whatever was in my future. My unscrupulous fling was a thing of the past.

Jean Valjean's unscrupulous deeds, though, were still in play. He was last seen moving on in the middle of the night with the stolen silver. Unfortunately for him, Valjean generally sucked at his getaways and he was caught as soon as the sun broke the horizon. The police brought the deflated criminal back to the bishop's house. But what you might expect to happen does not. The bishop's response is so beautiful, it makes me cry every time I read it.

> "Ah! Here you are!" he exclaimed, looking at Jean Valjean. "I am glad to see you. Well, but how is this? I gave you the candlesticks too, which are of silver like the rest, and for which you can certainly get two hundred francs. Why did you not carry them away with your forks and spoons?"
>
> Jean Valjean opened his eyes wide, and stared at the venerable Bishop with an expression which no human tongue can render any account of.
>
> "Monseigneur," said the brigadier of gendarmes, "so what this man said is true, then? We came across him. He was walking like a man who is running away. We stopped him to look into the matter. He had this silver—"
>
> "And he told you," interposed the Bishop with a smile, "that it had been given to him by a kind old fellow of a priest with whom he had passed the night? I see how the matter stands. And you have brought him back here? It is a mistake."
>
> "In that case," replied the brigadier, "we can let him go?"
>
> "Certainly," replied the Bishop.
>
> The gendarmes released Jean Valjean, who

> recoiled.
>
> "Is it true that I am to be released?" he said, in an almost inarticulate voice, and as though he were talking in his sleep.
>
> "Yes, thou art released; dost thou not understand?" said one of the gendarmes.
>
> "My friend," resumed the Bishop, "before you go, here are your candlesticks. Take them."
>
> He stepped to the chimney-piece, took the two silver candlesticks, and brought them to Jean Valjean ...
>
> Jean Valjean was trembling in every limb. He took the two candlesticks mechanically, and with a bewildered air.
>
> *Les Misérables*, Victor Hugo[5]

As soon as the police left, the bishop told Valjean he had redeemed him from a life of evil and had bought him for a life of good. After hearing the bishop's declaration, Valjean experienced a deep, inner turmoil. He wrestled with the "vile wretch"[6] that he had become and the grace that was so freely offered. When he emerged from the conflict, Jean Valjean was different. "That which was certain, that which he did not doubt, was that he was no longer the same man, that everything about him was changed, that it was no longer in his power to make it as though the Bishop had not spoken to him and had not touched him."[7]

Unfortunately, my own heart had not yet wrestled with the “vile wretch” I had become. I mistakenly thought I could continue dating Jerimiah as if nothing had ever happened.

Who could be all right with that?

Apparently me.

During Christmas break, Jerimiah and I sat with my parents in the living room, discussing our possible marriage that very summer.

But my duplicity finally caught up with me. Jerimiah is no moron. He knew something wasn't right. The truth began to emerge shortly after the New Year when he finally got the sordid story out of me over the phone. He was hurt, yes, but worse, the love he held for me in his heart was severed. He didn't just dump my sorry behind. He said he was done with me forever.

I was forced to come face-to-face with my hideous self. Even worse, I was left alone with her. Losing someone so precious forced me to acknowledge what I once had—as is often the case in life.

Devastated, I could barely function. You would've thought someone I loved had died. So it wasn't hard for me convince my professors of a supposed family emergency that would take me away from school for a few days. Without my parents' knowledge or consent, I borrowed my roommate's car and drove the four hours to Jerimiah's house. It was quite possibly the worst drive of my life.

I headed straight there before I had the chance to chicken out. Nothing could prepare me for what I found. His usually neat and carefully organized room had been turned upside-down. He was sitting on the floor in the midst of the rubble and, when his eyes finally met mine, *I* wanted to die. To witness the pain in his eyes was to suffer. But I deserved it, every blasted second of it plus a thousand times more. Never before had I felt such desperation to take back my actions. But as we are well aware, the clock does not rewind. Instead, it stood still.

In retrospect, I can't tell you how many days I was there or that I even ate or slept. What I do recall is spending countless hours answering Jerimiah's terse questions and often breaking his unflinching, angry gaze. Eventually though, I had to go back to school. So I gathered the shattered pieces of my own making and dragged my now single self back to the responsibilities of life. Without a doubt, it was one of the darkest periods I have ever faced.

Had our breakup been the end of things between us, I know with certainty I would be an altogether different person today—and not in a good way. But something beyond my ability to comprehend transpired within Jerimiah's heart, for he lived a life I'd not yet tasted and had a close relationship with God.

God was, for all practical purposes, his dad (Jerimiah had an unfair and woeful time of it in the earthly father department). And as much as he wanted to ignore the directive, he felt God clearly tell him to remain my friend and support me after our break up. The decree went something along the lines of, "Be there for her through this time."

It sounded absurd, but Jerimiah gave it his best shot.

I've sat, staring at the blinking cursor on my computer

screen for quite some time, pondering the next sequence of events. But it still does not make rational sense to me.

Jerimiah followed through and did what he felt God instructed him to do. As he did, he softened toward me. He forgave me. Astoundingly, the man whose heart I mutilated ended up being the man who believed I could be someone far better than a liar and a cheat. The love I had once been so careless with was revived. Still, I was surely not entitled to what came next.

Since we didn't get to see each other on a regular basis to know what the others' days were comprised of, he made me a candid video titled *The Life And Times of Jerimiah*. We sat down to watch it together on the evening of February 13, 1999. At the end of the video, he looked directly into the camera with his unflinching and adoring gaze and asked, "Beth, will you marry me?" Confused, I turned to the real-life Jerimiah and saw reflections of light dancing off the diamond he offered in his hands. The rest is, well, history.

As far as Jean Valjean's life is concerned, his misdeeds were history. He was new and improved; a changed man. As you can imagine, after the grace shown to him, he did much good with the remainder of his life: Helped plenty of undeserving people. Re-vitalized an entire town. Rescued and raised the orphan Cosette as his daughter. Protected and freed the police inspector Javert, who ruthlessly hunted him for years. And saved his future son-in-law Marius' life, though Marius didn't know it at the time. The old bishop's gift made a deep and lasting impact on Valjean, and Valjean followed in the bishop's footsteps.

Except for one thing. Valjean still regarded himself as an unworthy, wretched convict. Once Cosette married Marius and had a new protector, Valjean's conscience compelled him to inform Marius of his sordid past and distance himself from the pair.

But Valjean told Marius only the *bad* parts of his history. And he begged Marius to keep everything from Cosette. The contact between convict father and newlyweds dwindled to non-existent.

To Valjean, this separation was like the removal of air. Cosette was his entire life and joy. He began to die without her. By the time Marius put all the pieces of Valjean's life together, it was almost too late. The couple raced to his side and found him on his deathbed. The last few pages of Valjean's story are bittersweet. He was reunited with his beloved Cosette and knew enormous happiness. But his malady was too far gone and he died. End of story.

Well, just how has the new and improved Beth done? I've tried my best to be a wife worthy of the man I married. Trustworthy. Honest. Loyal. I think I've done a decent job. But oftentimes I feel like I still exist beneath the shadow of my crime. And its weight can be crushing, especially since I never endured the full punishment.

I alternate between defensiveness and fear. The fact my cheating days are a distant, albeit painful, memory doesn't matter. The truth is: I cheated on Jerimiah. I could become the quintessential wife and *still* not be able to take back my folly. I'll always have that black mark on my record; hence the defensiveness. And the fear kicks in when I wonder, *Who am I to deserve Jerimiah's love or any shred of happiness with him?* What I *should* have is the antithesis of what I *actually* have. It becomes a struggle to believe the considerable grace he gave me.

Here is my overarching concern: that my ending will be like Valjean's. Don't get me wrong. The reborn Jean Valjean was certainly a man to emulate. That doesn't change the fact he died earlier than he should have, due to a broken heart (an affliction found rarely in real life). Why didn't Valjean simply tell Marius his entire story? The bad *with* the good? Then he would've lived out the rest of his days sheltered in the love of his children. It's what they all wanted. The problem: I don't think Valjean allowed himself to be *fully* transformed by grace. I say that because I believe there's more to this confounding gift than meets the eye.

> He had been almost a villain and had become almost a saint; and after being chained with prison irons he was still fettered with a chain that was scarcely less onerous although invisible, that of his prison record. The law had never lost its claim on him.
>
> *Les Misérables*, Victor Hugo[8]

My theory is as follows. The gift of grace comes with an accessory. Freedom. This means the gift remains only partially opened—in all its beautifully-wrapped packaging—until the recipient starts to live with the understanding that they can, in fact, be truly free.

• • •

The Holy Spirit and I are on the move again, slowly descending down the rugged rock face. Our conversation is jovial as we banter back and forth.

A shadow passes over and I tilt my head back to identify the disturbance. A fluffy white cloud floats by on a cool breeze. Perfectly rounded edges make it look like the epitome of a cartoon drawing—a careless, meandering, happy little cloud.

But it's not alone. Groups of cauliflower-shaped clouds loom large in the distance, as if they are an approaching army pursuing the fluffy, ill-fated scout. My eyes grow round and troubled at the gray army's menacing approach. Suddenly the wind hurls a cold, violent thrust in our direction.

"Um, it looks like a storm is coming." I try to keep my voice light so I won't betray my mounting concern. "What's the plan for rain?" And wind, and possibly other, more terrible things ... I conjure up images of my klutzy fingers losing their grip on the descender and my face slamming into the hard stones after my feet slide helplessly off.

The Holy Spirit is not fooled by my falsely light tone. "Stick close to Me. We'll ride it out together." His voice is strong and confident.

I'm unable to contain my trepidation. "*What?*" My voice

raises an octave. "That's *it*? *That's* Your master plan?"

His face reflects chagrin over my doubts and He answers with a neutral "Yes."

My terror takes over as I look about with wide eyes, searching for some way to ride out the impending doom safely.

He does not know what He's talking about! There's no way I'm going to hang here, suspended in mid-air, who knows how high above the ground, and ride out the storm that blew Dorothy and Toto to Oz!

In that moment, my eyes come to rest on something I hadn't noticed before. To my left, the rock face abruptly turns a corner and recedes and, from there, continues on in a similar straight line. Just after the recession, and slightly lower down, I see a tiny ledge with a slight natural granite overhang ... and a lone figure, who looks very much like Theb.

What is she doing there? How did she get down?

I muse over these and several other questions before a monstrous peal of thunder sounds, making me jump. I glance behind me and remember the approaching army gaining on us. I whip my head back to look at the Holy Spirit. He wears a far off expression, appearing to be in deep, calculating thought. His lips move silently as if He is speaking to Himself. I don't think He's paying any attention to me.

Without conscious thought as to what I am doing, I creep to where the rock face juts back. I peer cautiously at the Holy Spirit with each inch. He doesn't seem to notice. I take advantage of His apparent preoccupation and disappear around the corner.

My rope keeps getting tangled; it is meant only for descent, not horizontal creeping. I continue to loosen my descender and clutch for handholds in the protruding rocks as I grow closer to Theb and the safe ledge. I can see her more clearly now, excitedly leaning toward the edge of the miniscule shelf and waving me over.

Abruptly, a drop of rain hits my outstretched calf like the first cannon shot signaling the commencement of battle. With a fierce bellow, a volley of raindrops are released and, in an instant, I am soaked. My drenched arms and legs grasp at the slick granite as I painstakingly work my way to cover. I finally edge close enough for Theb to reach out and guide me to safety. In my relief to set my feet on something solid, I cautiously grab her in a one-armed hug. She returns it, joyfully squeezing me in welcome.

She looks normal, unlike the last time I remember seeing her. But I'm not about to bring *that* up. "How did you get here?" I ask in wonder.

Theb's smirk is huge. "I found my own gear. I don't listen to what *He* says." Her words drip bitterness. "Someone had to keep you safe—right?"

My reply is stolen by the great gust of wind that slams into us, nearly knocking me back off the ledge. I grab on to the nearest handhold I can find to steady my quaking legs.

I'm close to exhaustion after the combination of my horizontal rock climb and struggle with the violent storm. The ridge is much smaller than it appeared from a distance now that it's housing both of us. I wonder, a little belatedly, which of us would be left standing if push came to shove.

I glance at Theb, who is in a similar tenuous position. She looks a bit startled—as if she hadn't factored in the ramifications of us both being on the same slippery ledge. I can feel the confidence over my rash decision drain systematically from my body.

What have I done? Where is the Holy Spirit?

I squint through the rain, back in the direction I came from, and realize I can't see Him anymore.

He was so confident in His plan, but I didn't believe Him. Now that I'm here, in my definition of safe and sound, I don't feel any better. Theb's panicked presence only serves as fuel for the inferno of my distressed thoughts. Fear claws at me, threatening to break my hold on the weather-beaten rocks.

"So," Theb says. "What do we do?"

I turn and gawk at her, alarmed. "I don't know!"

Theb arches a brow and her eyes become hard slivers. "Then why did you scurry over here?" Her tone is acid.

I am startled by her question. "Because it looked—" I cut myself off and cock my head to one side. "Why am I explaining myself to you? Didn't you say something earlier about keeping *me* safe?"

She bites her lower lip and looks away before responding. "Well, what I really meant to say is ... that I ... uh ... just wanted to keep tabs on you."

"You were *spying* on me? Ugh." My nose wrinkles with disdain. "How creepy!"

Theb sputters. "Oh yeah? ... Well you just left me. To be with Him! What did you expect me to do? It's not like I have anywhere else to go." Her voice becomes petulant. "Now poor, widdle Beffie comes cwaling back." She flashes me a derisive smile and laughs. "I knew you'd desert Him at some point. It was only a matter of time."

I inhale sharply, horrified by her words. "I didn't desert him! I mean—I did, sort of. But it wasn't because ..." I trail off, then try again. "I panicked. I wasn't consciously aware of what I was doing. Surely He won't hold that against me." Lightning illuminates the darkened day and low rumbles of thunder follow close on its heels.

"Oh pul-eeze!" Theb now has to shout over the noise. "If He's anything like me," she raises her eyebrows meaningfully, "you'd have to grovel for a long while in order to get back in His good graces."

A cold gust of wind chooses this moment to articulate her point and again threaten our precarious perch on the ledge. I feel my blood turn to ice at her statement.

"Don't you see?" she yells. "He was only putting up with you because you agreed to take the fall with Him. He's nice. He could see how badly you wanted to please Him and He felt *sorry* for you." She sneers. "But there's an end to His good-guy routine. I mean, He already rescued you once. You're not worth Him coming to find again."

I nod mutely as her words sink in.

She's right. I am a coward. And a deserter. He deserves better. He deserves someone who will actually listen and trust what he says. I'm such an idiot! I lost my chance of being with Him.

I've never felt more alone. Or hollow. I turn my face to

meet the sideways rain. The stinging needles are relentless as they mingle with the tears now streaming down my cheeks. The ledge offers no protection from the raging tempest. I am worse off than before because I am not directly beneath a taut line. If I slip, I will be chewed up by the rocks as my rope seeks to correct and straighten its course.

I stand next to Theb, shivering, resigned to my unknown yet dismal future. We remain silent for a time.

Then a new sound—something altogether different from the loud claps of thunder and pelting rain—slowly enters my consciousness. It has a deep timbre and resembles a voice.

It's calling my name?

I strain to hear against the bedlam. It *is* my name! My eyes squint to locate the source and I see the Holy Spirit. He's lower than me now, to my right, near the corner I turned to get over to the ledge.

I watch as He cups His hands to His mouth and calls my name again. My heart stutters and beats faster. I can tell Theb spots Him when I hear her gasp. For once, she seems speechless—and I am grateful. I realize I no longer care what Theb thinks. I only feel the wonder and elation coursing through my veins over the fact that He has apparently come to find me.

My internal celebration ends abruptly. *He must have come to find me because He is angry.* He's too far away to read His facial expression, but that can be His only reason—I'm sure of it. I certainly don't blame Him. After all, who wants to be around a cowering sissy who obviously doesn't believe you? But at least, it seems, I'll have a chance to grovel.

Maybe I can earn back His favor. One thing I know for sure. Being reunited with Theb is not where I want or need to be.

I gather my courage and force it directly down my leg into my foot, taking a tentative step off of the ledge. Once my hands find their hold, my other foot follows. I feel Theb put a hand of warning on my shoulder, but I shrug it off. I am too preoccupied with my risky descent to care about any further arguments from her.

My slack line is a constant reminder of my perilous position; the entrenched storm does not lessen its attack. In order to see, I am forced to narrow my eyes against the water pouring down my face.

I chance a glance down and realize that I am, in fact, drawing closer to the Holy Spirit's position. I feel some small victory over my accomplishment, but know it's not yet the time for celebration. I am more concerned with the growing fatigue in my aching limbs. Each new position I take on the rock face seems to sap more strength.

When I feel I can go no further, I stop to locate the Holy Spirit. I see He is reasonably close. With great effort, I rally my muscles to give a final advance. I move my right foot down and find a toe-hold. My left foot follows but, with the balance shift, my right foot loses its grip.

Time slows as I watch my feet fly out from underneath me; my knees slam into the rough granite. I cry out in pain and horror as my body swings out and I plummet downward and to the right—the route my rope must take to straighten. My arms and legs scramble for a way to stop my plunge while being mercilessly ground and torn by the sharp rocks. I make out a blur of gray and grit just before my head slams into the stone.

Without warning, I come to a screeching halt. I wince against the final blow of pain I expect to follow, but there is none. When I attempt to cautiously reach up to make sure my skull is still in one piece I realize my arm is pinned.

I look up through the rain to find a set of concerned eyes on mine. The Holy Spirit holds me tight in His grasp and gives me a sad smile as His eyes seem to take inventory of my wounds. I am too overwhelmed with pain and exhaustion to do anything other than close my eyes and sag onto His chest. I succumb to the growing blackness.

I awaken to a peculiar quiet. As I crack my eyes open, I realize the silence is due to a lack of wind and rain. My next observation startles me. I am lying on my back.

I sit up with a gasp—ignoring the throbbing sensation my hasty movement creates—and look around. I appear to be on some sort of small bluff. There are boulders around an open space and even clusters of trees dotting this new landscape. A merry fire crackles next to me, warming my chilled body and the damp ground.

How did I get here?

Just then, I hear a rustle, and I turn to see the Holy Spirit walk out from among the boulders—more firewood in hand. He joins me next to the fire.

"Good," He says. "You're awake. How do you feel?" His concern is evident in His tone.

I feel His eyes on me, but fail to meet His gaze. "F—f—fine." I pause, not knowing how to say what I'm thinking.

"Uh, thanks for, you know, stopping my fall."

"You're welcome."

"Where are we?" I ask.

"We're not too far below our position from before the storm. I originally planned for us to make our way down here to ride it out. We wouldn't have had any cover, but our feet would've been on terra firma."

I eye Him for some clue as to what He's thinking. He doesn't appear angry, but I'm not eager to speak. I catch a glimpse of grief in His bottomless gaze.

I clear my suddenly arid throat. "Listen, I'm really sorry for taking off like that. I got scared and I—um—didn't really think about what I was doing. I'm sorry you had to come after me again." I inhale deeply, gathering oxygen for some serious groveling when His voice cuts me off.

"I forgive you."

My eyes snap to His in disbelief, but I see only truth conveyed. The traces of His earlier grief have vanished.

"Oh!" I say, flustered. Then I compose myself and reply humbly, "Thank You." Again I pause, sorting out my tangled thoughts. "How long till You leave?"

He arches an eyebrow. "Where am I going?"

I shrug. "I don't know. I just figured You wouldn't want to be around me anymore after ... after ..."

"Why would I leave?"

I look down. "I realize you have forgiven me. But aren't there—" I swallow thickly. "—consequences to my actions?"

He lifts my chin up and nods. "But they're not what you think."

He points to the blood-encrusted scrapes and rapidly forming bruises marking my body. "Did *I* wound you?"

I shake my head no.

"Those are a result of you doing what you thought best instead of trusting Me. *Those* are the consequences of your actions. I'm not out to get you, you know. I didn't get a kick out of seeing you tumble down the side of the mountain. Look ..." He pauses. "I'm not like the fictitious gods the Greeks believed in, waiting for you to screw up so I can scourge and kill you. And I am most certainly *not* looking for an excuse to desert you at the first sign of your poor choices."

"Well I know that—"

"You *think* you know it," He interrupts. "Yet you believe I would abandon you after I *promised* never to leave you—no matter what you do."

"I know You *said* that. But I deserve to get left! Surely there's a limit to Your promise: some line that, once crossed, sends me past the point of no return." I pause. "Maybe ... maybe this wasn't the thing that pushed me over the edge. But I need to know what that *thing* is."

He heaves a great sigh. "You're having quite a difficult time accepting grace. My unmerited favor." He muses to Himself, "How can I put it so you'll fully receive what I'm saying?" He turns His eyes to mine. "You know I love you, right?" I blink then nod.

"And you're aware that I've *always* loved you, even though you've done nothing to earn My love?"

My "Mmh-hmm" sounds through closed lips.

"Did you believe you would somehow become perfect?"

He asks. I slowly shake my head back and forth. "You believe you must somehow earn My grace—but grace can't be earned. It's a gift that I've already given you."

"Love seems so much simpler," I mumble. "Grace is hard. It doesn't make sense to me."

The Holy Spirit's rebuttal is swift yet gentle. "I'm not asking you to understand it." He pauses. "If someone wanted to give you a watch, would you figure out how it worked before you'd accept it?"

I smile reluctantly. "Well when you put it *that* way ..."

"If you will believe the truth of My grace, instead of attempting to dissect it, you'll find freedom."

"Freedom?" I ask.

"Yep. I don't want you to go through your life approaching Me the same way you would a depraved dictator—constant fear that you'll do something wrong mixed with the subsequent terror of punishment. That's not the life I've called you to live. Any discipline or rebuke you'll receive from Me is because I love you and I want to correct your behavior. My grace gives you the freedom to get to know Me and thrive in My love. You'll learn to stop living like an escaped convict in hiding."

His mouth curves up in a sideways grin. "Besides, I don't mind you being in awe of Me and the gifts I give. I'm *all* about lopsided relationships you know," He says with a twinkle in His eye.

"No doubt," I mumble.

I shift my weight and am painfully reminded of my wounds.

I wince before saying, “So ... I know You didn’t cause me to become dirty and bloodied, but I was wondering if ... um ... You might be able to help me get fixed up?”

“It sure took you long enough to ask.” He offers me a smile. “That's one of the reasons I'm here. You know, helping you clean up is a specialty of Mine.” He winks and I watch as He grabs a first aid kit from our supplies and goes to work cleaning my wounds.

“I believe You,” I blurt out. “I mean,” I hesitate. “I know I'm not getting what I deserve.” I shake my head gingerly back and forth. “But I can’t live a life good enough to pay You back for Your grace. And I think—” I swallow, “I think You're telling me I don't have to?” I ask, hopeful.

“That’s *exactly* what I'm saying.” He leans over and gently wipes the quiet tears from my cheeks.

• Chapter 7 •
An Acute Case of the Marthas

My body wanted a baby. I felt empty and I wanted to be full. I wanted someone to love who would stay: stay and be there, always. And I wanted Henry to be in this child, so that when he was gone he wouldn't be entirely gone, there would be a bit of him with me ... insurance, in case of fire, flood, act of God.

The Time Traveler's Wife, Audrey Niffenegger[1]

One day, after a particularly awful argument with Jerimiah, I peeled my car out of the driveway and drove aimlessly, trying to clear my head and sob in solitude. With the vivid colors of autumn whizzing by, I turned down a country road and passed a large white house with a No Trespassing sign posted. It was so intriguing I slammed on my brakes and turned around in the parking lot of a rustic convenience store.

I drove back to the house and led my car onto the circular driveway; my tires crunching on debris lining the dilapidated concrete. Ignoring the unlawful entry warning situated amid slowly creeping vines, I got out of my car, quietly shut the door, and set off to explore the ample grounds. A large, unfinished brick fountain stood stoically on the front lawn. I could see hints of an in-ground pool and decorative brick fencing in the back yard. My attention, however, was riveted to the looming structure encased in oversized vinyl siding.

This two-story, Charleston-style home had a front porch spanning nearly the entire length of the top and bottom floors. At one time, this home was the centerpiece of a dignified country estate. But now it stood bereft of its former glory because it had been gutted by a fire.

The scorched structure echoed my gloomy mood, so I continued on in my perusal. I could tell the fire started on the left side of the house—that was the area standing as an exposed skeleton. The scant amount of surviving siding was melted and sagging. Through an upper window, I spotted a rather haunting image: a burnt staircase illuminated by a gaping hole in the charred roof remains.

In my mind's eye, it was as if I were watching a movie sequence shot in slow motion, depicting the former life within the walls of the house. I visualized a little girl, her blond curls streaming behind her as she raced to beat her brother up the stairs. Their fading laughter seemed to echo all around the melted structure. *How sad,* I thought. *The house can no longer serve the purpose it was created for—to harbor life. It's a worthless shell.*

And then it dawned on me—the reason I was so compelled to turn around and inspect this place despite fear of arrest or death by neighborly shotgun. *I can relate to this house*—for my foul mood went *far* beyond a horrible argument with my husband. In that moment, my heart felt scorched and vacant, devoid of anything worthwhile. The fires had seen to that. Plural fires, for no singular blaze was responsible for my heart's devastation.

What fires?

The fires of life: failure, loss, disappointment, fatigue, heartache, pain, fear, confusion, doubt, grief, anxiety, broken dreams, hopelessness ... I could go on for a while. Each foe strikes a match and hurls it straight at the heart. These fires are started very early in the human existence and show no partiality to race, gender, or economic status. While the resulting flames are most often eventually extinguished, the damage is done. My own heart had been consumed by fire after fire until all that was left was a pile of overgrown skeletal remains.

And just when I thought the parallels between me and this house could be no more apt, I walked around to the other side, the one with the *least* amount of damage. I stopped dead in my tracks and stared at it, taken aback by what I saw.

A six-foot-wide hole had been cut out of the exterior wall into what had once been either a dining room or a family room. The neatly hewn hole wasn't the bizarre part, given the state of the rest of the house. The four gigantic bales of hay presently occupying the space inside, however, unsettled me. *What in the world?*

Naturally, in writing this, I did a little research on hay. It must be kept completely free of moisture. So, when resources permit, hay can be stored under a roof—*typically* in the form of a barn. I guess this charred mansion was the exception. It seemed that it was only good for one thing: a storehouse for livestock feed. Might as well make the skeleton useful, right?

Those bales of hay got me chewing on some meaty questions about myself as I drove away from the charred house remains: #1. What or who *exactly* is my heart created to house? #2. Was my heart a complete loss? It didn't take an insurance adjuster to realize the house standing before me was deemed exactly that. And #3. Was my heart equivalent to the dining room-turned-hay storage? Meaning: is it possible my heart was amassing and housing a pathetic counterfeit to what it *should* be storing?

My answers came in a jumbled up order.

In my middle school bus-riding days, my friend and I made up a song. Well, actually, we changed the lyrics to an at-the-time-popular song as we shoved trash into the back of the torn bus seat directly in front of our assigned one.

♪ *There's a hole in the seat that can on-ly be filled wi-th trash.* ♫

We were so clever. We filled that sucker too. Gum. Candy wrappers. Notebook paper. Jimmy Hoffa's body. Everything and anything we could get our hands on made it into that crevice. Our bus driver would try to cap the illegal dumping by plastering duct tape all over the back of the seat. But duct tape can't stop two girls with fingernails and endless amounts of time. (Growing up, I lived out in the country, which made for a drawn-out bus ride.) It didn't take long for the material covering the seats to start bulging from the rubble within.

Unfortunately, I carried my bus-seat-stuffing habit into real life. I've spent a lot of time trying to fill up on things that were never meant to satisfy. For as long as I can remember, I've struggled with over-eating. I'm not a large person by design and I've never really gotten to a point where most of America would label me fat. But I have some seriously chunky pictures, which seem to span the last decade or so. I have to work really hard to rid my upper thighs of the bit of cottage cheese that never used to be there. I'm also struggling to shed the upper arm dangle usually presenting itself in elderly church organists.

My problem: I can never get enough. I always want more good food to put into my mouth. While my belly is screaming for me to halt, my taste buds are hollering for more. I don't have to have a bad day in order to stuff myself like a Thanksgiving turkey. When Jerimiah and I hang out with friends, I don't even consider it fun unless food is part of the equation. The worst part about my deranged need is, when I've finally reached the point of having to put on elastic pants, I feel emptier than before I started.

I haven't begun to touch the surface of my staggering requirements though. Sometimes I feel like a black hole. I'm always searching for what will make me feel complete, so I suck in everything around me (this extends well past my Twilight and all-things-romance obsession). It's almost like I'm afraid to be alone with my thoughts. I can't even manage simple tasks without background noise. I fold laundry with the TV on. Housecleaning is completed with my iPhone strapped to my arm and music blaring in my ears. If I'm in my car for more than five minutes, I must find someone to call for conversation.

But the present is not my only issue. I look to future events to sustain me. My mindset has typically been: *I will feel better when ________ occurs.*

A classic example of mine: Jerimiah and I are usually able to travel to Florida for Christmas to spend time with a large portion of both families. I'll spend the four months prior to our trip excitedly wishing the time away and fantasizing about all the exceptional moments we will share with our loved ones. I envision both our families sitting around one *huge* table in a make-believe mansion with presents piled crazy-high around the Christmas tree. (At this point, you can see I've already exited reality.)

In my vision, we are all cracking up over the same joke as the strains of bright Christmas music are heard coming from Dad's turntable. (There's no better sound than the intermittent crackling of a record.) Everyone is getting along and even the imaginary dog is polite in his begging. Once our fabulous zero-calorie feast is finished, we play games like Balderdash and Scattergories long into the night, having more fun together than humanly possible.

In my mystical Christmas reverie, there is no arguing, whining, frustration, annoyance, or selfishness. There is only sheer delight, love, and endless laughter.

Don't get me wrong—we always have a great time. But, without fail, when we return home, I am left scratching my head and wondering why our trip didn't make me feel *all better.*

Another future event I attempt to find contentment in is starting a family with Jerimiah. And after recently reading the seemingly mocking and heartless words "Not Pregnant" at the other end of a pee-stick, I became very upset. Right then I decided I would like to invent a new line of home pregnancy tests—at least for those women who *desire* to be with child. The test would of course read "Pregnant" for those who are expecting. I'd even throw a "Congratulations" on it too.

The negative indicator is more complicated because my two ideas would surely force manufacturers to enlarge the digital display. Regardless, I am somewhere between "Sorry, Please Try Again" and "Keep Practicing—Your Day Will Come." I'm not saying my heart would pound any less while I wait for the results, but maybe I would feel a diminished devastation upon reading an apologetic or encouraging no.

I was stumped as to why the words "Not Pregnant" affected me so negatively. It's not like Jerimiah and I had been trying to get pregnant for a long time. Heck, we only stopped using birth control within the last several years while maintaining the mindset of "whatever happens, happens."

Then I had a revelation. I've secretly wanted to get pregnant for a long time. Every supposed scare throughout our marriage led me to a hidden hope God overrode my birth control and conjured up a bun to place in my oven. Since I am no longer popping birth control pills, this underground hope is raised to heightened levels. So any slight inconsistencies I notice with my body cause me to believe I *could* be pregnant. Almost instantly I get sucked into the hopes and dreams of motherhood. I start picking out names, making cool crochet stuffed animals, and praying for my child's future spouse. I guess it's perfectly natural for me to feel a little hollow once I discover my oven hasn't even been pre-heated.

I digress. Remember my middle-school-bus-seat-stuffing-buddy? The song we altered was "Hole Hearted" by Extreme. I looked up the music video on YouTube and cracked up over the spandex shorts and only-slightly-smaller-than-the-80's man hair. Aside from that, the *real* lyrics are fairly legitimate. They talk about circles and squares and how one can't fit in a space shaped like the other. About how the author has a heart-hole that can't be filled with anything or anyone but the person he's writing the song to.

I've obviously attempted to fill my heart with a number of different people and things over the years: Husband. Mom. Dad. Grandparents. Future children. Brothers. Sisters-in-law. Aunts and uncles. Cousins. New friends. Old friends. Lifelong friends. My dog. Making crafts. Good food. Exercise. Reading. Swimming. Movies. Enjoying beautiful sights all around me. Working with kids at church.

As good as these people and things are, as much as they mean to me, I cannot escape the gnawing ache of emptiness haunting me when I am alone with my thoughts. It turns out my answer to question #3 is a resounding "yes." My busyness and distractions are merely an excuse to not have to deal with my burnt-out dining-room-turned-storage-facility-for-hay.

> Keep your heart with all vigilance, for from it flow the springs of life.
>
> Proverbs 4:23[2]

This brings me right back to my first question. Who or what was my heart created to house? Before I answer, let me first get past an obnoxious issue. We all know the *brain* is the organ responsible for our emotions. Yet, poetically speaking, we give the heart this distinction. Why? Because, in the ancient world, the heart was defined as the inner man (or woman) and the seat of spiritual life.[3] Apparently, even as scientific understanding evolved, the idea still stuck.

The Latin word for heart is *cor* or *cordis*.[4] Our English word "core" describes the center or most essential part of anything.[5] As incorrect as the ancients were about human physiology, they at least understood that the seat of spiritual life and the inner person are at the very core of the human existence.

At the heart of the matter.

Now here's the part where people may disagree with me; that's okay since I have no science to back me up in this regard. No physical proof.

That being said, I believe my heart was created to be Jesus Christ's dwelling place, His abode. This is not a physical distinction. It's a spiritual one. Jesus crafted my heart so precisely to fit Him—the builder—that anything else is strange and uncomfortable. It's true. A square cannot fit where a circle belongs.

And substitutions can be disastrous ...

During one of the first visits our now long-time friends Kevin and Hannah made to our house, I decided to make low-carb brownies. Having gained a few comfortably-married pounds, Jerimiah and I were in our Atkins diet phase. Being the opposite of adventurous in the kitchen, I had never before attempted a baking recipe from scratch. But, low and behold, a Hershey bar I unearthed from a hiding place deep in the recesses of the cupboard had a brownie recipe on the label. So I whipped the ingredients together making some *minor* substitutions so it could become low-carb, and proudly stacked the delicious-smelling delicacies on a plate.

With a flourish, I served everyone a huge brownie topped with a scoop of low-carb vanilla ice cream. I went back to the kitchen to get my own piece when I became aware of a peculiar silence emanating from the living room, followed by stifled giggling. Choking back laughter, Jerimiah hollered to me asking if I had tasted the brownies yet.

I had not.

I couldn't even be upset at his amusement once I chewed my first revolting bite. The brownies were a chalky version of how cow poo must taste (notice I said *must*, not *does*). I'm not sure which *exact* substitution sealed their fate but I know it was a horrible attempt on my part. One which I am still trying to live down years later.

On a spiritual level, I had been feeding my soul everything *but* God, hoping the ingredients I was substituting would suffice. But my soul substitutions were proving to be even more wretched than the brownies. It seemed if I wanted my soul to absorb what was good, I would *have* to cut out the substitutes. Replace them with the real thing.

I believe my point is corroborated in the Bible by an encounter Jesus had with two sisters who seemed to be friends of His. Enter: Martha and Mary.

> Now as they went on their way, Jesus entered a village. And a woman named Martha welcomed him into her house. And she had a sister called Mary, who sat at the Lord's feet and listened to his teaching. But Martha was distracted with much serving.
>
> Luke 10:38-40a[6]

The Bible isn't clear about exactly how many people were with Jesus, but I think it's safe to say there was quite a crowd in Mary and Martha's home. Perhaps it was mealtime and the crowd was anxiously waiting on their pita chips and hummus with a side dish of olives.

Somewhere along the way I decided Martha was a disagreeable and altogether unlikable woman who probably sported a unibrow. I visualize her in the kitchen, muttering angrily under her breath about Mary's laziness as she prepared the legumes for the large pot of soup she was working on.

I believe Martha mentally amassed her list of complaints regarding her sister: *Mary is forever leaving her dirty tunics on the nearest stool and can't grind barley to save her life!*

Her frustration grew as her guests' stomachs rumbled. Finally, Martha—armed with her erupting anger, disheveled hair, and lentil-covered apron—marched into the room where Jesus sat in order to tell on Mary.

> And she went up to him and said, "Lord, do you not care that my sister has left me to serve alone? Tell her then to help me." But the Lord answered her, "Martha, Martha, you are anxious and troubled about many things, but one thing is necessary. Mary has chosen the good portion, which will not be taken away from her."
>
> Luke10:40b-42[7]

I usually grin with delight as Jesus puts Martha in her place. He totally gives her the smack-down. However, I think I may have been missing the point. Why *wasn't* Mary helping her dear-old unibrowed sister?

Well, she was otherwise engaged. Mary was sitting at the Lord's feet, listening to what He said. She allowed herself to be captivated and filled by His words. Listening to Him seemed fundamental to her existence. I don't know what kind of figurative fires-of-the-heart this sister endured, but she was not storing any hay in her dining room *or* stuffing trash into her bus seat. She was commissioning the best and only carpenter capable of restoring her charred heart—the One who built it to begin with. Jesus said she chose what was *better*. And it would not be taken away from her.

> *Satisfy* us in the morning with your steadfast love, that we may rejoice and be glad all our days.
>
> Psalm 90:14[8]

• • •

The cheery fire crackles and pops, casting shadows into the darkening twilight. The Holy Spirit and I sit across the flames from each other. He says we will make camp and sleep here tonight. As I am wearied from our day so far, the prospect of rest and warmth greatly appeals to me.

I let out a huge, contented sigh as I lean back onto my elbows. "I am soooo glad to not have to move right now—I'm stinkin' tired!" My stomach growls loudly, making us both chuckle.

"I guess I'm a bit hungry too. Well. Maybe that means I've been burning a lot of calories today—and that's a great thing! In fact, I need to input this in my phone so I can keep track."

I fish my iPhone from my pocket. I open the Lose It app and frown in concentration. "How many calories do you think I've burned so far? I'm thinking that if *anyone* would know my exact amount, it would be You," I say with a grin.

The Holy Spirit flashes an amused smile at me. "Yes, I do know, but—"

I hold up my hand to stop Him as I distractedly type on my phone. "Wait—never mind. I just estimated."

I mash the standby button and set the phone on the ground beside me. “Can You believe my app had orienteering as an exercise and not rappelling? What in the heck is orienteering? Oh well, doesn’t matter.”

“You’re really focused on counting those calories,” He comments.

“Yeah, I’ve been working hard.” My smile is a proud one. “Thanks for noticing.”

He raises an eyebrow. “How could I *not* notice? It’s all you’ve been concentrating on the past few minutes.”

I frown. “What are You getting at?”

“Don't you think there's more to life?” He asks.

I’m immediately defensive. “Well of course there is! My fitness and eating aren't the only things I think about! But I want to feel and look good, especially for Jerimiah!” I cock my head and stare at Him pointedly. “In fact, shouldn't it make You *happy* that I want my husband to find me attractive?”

“Of course it does. But it’s not like you stop there. You gauge your fulfillment based on how you eat and what you look like on any given day.” He sighs. “That’s not all, either.”

I want to argue with Him but He speaks again before I have a chance to open my mouth.

“You've *always* looked at friends, family, circumstances and, heck, even the weather to sustain you. And when those things let you down—which they *all* inevitably do—you fall to pieces and walk around in a haze of depression.”

I eye Him warily and chew on my lip as His words bounce around in my head.

"Oh who am I kidding," I say abruptly. "You're right." The rock I had been fiddling with falls to the dirt as I promptly burst into tears. "I'm miserable. I'm basically a walking disaster."

The Holy Spirit slides over to sit by my side and puts an arm around me. With tears still flowing, I lay my head on His shoulder and accept His comfort. We sit quietly for a time before His voice breaks the silence.

"By the way, I know what you're thinking, and the answer is no."

"No what?" I manage between pitiful whimpers.

"It's not a total loss. Your heart *is* salvageable. Just look at Solomon for goodness sake. You're not nearly as forgone."

I sniffle loudly. "What does *Solomon* have to do with me?" I ask. "He had, like, a billion wives and was really wise. I only have my associate's degree and I most certainly do *not* swing that way."

He bursts out laughing. "Thanks for clearing that up," He says dryly. "Have you read Ecclesiastes?"

"Not much," I say. "What I've skimmed through seemed pretty depressing."

The Holy Spirit snorts in agreement. "I'll give you that one. Solomon had pretty much everything a human being could want: power, wealth, wisdom, love, but all that wasn't enough to satisfy his restless heart. He didn't deny himself any pleasure he wanted. He worked hard and was rewarded with joy. Yet, when he examined all he built and struggled to achieve, he realized, 'all was vanity and a striving after wind, and there was nothing to be gained under the sun.'[9] But

Solomon didn't end his appraisal there." I feel the Holy Spirit's breath move my hair.

"Vanity of vanities, says the Preacher, vanity of vanities! All is vanity. What does man gain by all the toil at which he toils under the sun? A generation goes, and a generation comes, but the earth remains forever. The sun rises, and the sun goes down, and hastens to the place where it rises. The wind blows to the south and goes around to the north; around and around goes the wind, and on its circuits the wind returns. All streams run to the sea, but the sea is not full; to the place where the streams flow, there they flow again. *All things are full of weariness; a man cannot utter it; the eye is not satisfied with seeing, nor the ear filled with hearing*. What has been is what will be, and what has been done is what will be done, and there is nothing new under the sun. Is there a thing of which it is said, 'See, this is new?' It has been already in the ages before us. There is no remembrance of former things, nor will there be any remembrance of later things yet to be among those who come after."[10]

I wipe my face with my sleeve. "No offense, but how *exactly* is that supposed to make me feel better?"

He gives my shoulder a squeeze before dropping His arm to turn and face me. "It goes to show you that one of the most powerful men to ever exist could have *everything* and still feel about life the way you do right now. You can have it all and it still won't be enough. The things you hold onto so tightly, thinking they're an answer to your emptiness, well, they're no more than God-Splenda."

"Say what?" A small smile spreads on my face. "I didn't know You came in convenient yellow packets."

His grin splits His face. "Nice. But that's just it—I don't." He looks thoughtful for a moment. "Speaking of the artificial, do you remember the bee you had a one-sided conversation with? You know, that time you sat in your backyard trying to write?"

My eyes flit back and forth as I recall what He's talking about. Then I bust out laughing.

"How funny," I laugh again. "And a little embarrassing that You know I was talking to a bee ... I do remember it though. The dang thing annoyed me. It was circling my Diet Cherry Pepsi like it was the most fragrant flower it had ever seen."

I shake my head back and forth with the memory. "It must've been confused. I thought bees were more intelligent than to go for straight up aspartame."

"Did you make fun of her—the bee—a little?" He asks, probing.

My nostrils flare as I breathe out with amused sarcasm. "Oh my word! Are You getting on my case for making fun of a *bee*?"

He suppresses a smile and holds up a hand in protest. "By no means am I saying that. It's just that she was *bee*-having more wisely than you gave her credit for."

"That was *so* corny," I say with a half-smile. "Fine. What was she doing then, if she wasn't chugging my diet cherry cola?"

"I'm sure you're aware that a bee's obvious choice of food

is nectar from a flower. They will, however, ingest sodas and other sugary syrups if nectar can't be found."

He pauses. "Now, in case you didn't know, bees can smell, but they *cannot* read. So in your backyard, the little worker knew *something* smelled good, but couldn't quite make the label out in order to know the contents included aspartame instead of real sugar. Until she did the bee-quivalent of sticking out her tongue to test it."[11]

I can't help but smile before saying, "So You're saying she didn't ingest any and take it back to her hive?"

"Nope. She was simply taste testing. The worker bee was designed to determine the difference between that which is artificial and that which brings life and can sustain her hive. So the bee left your drink alone to search for the real thing." I meet His gaze. "You were designed to do the same ... on a spiritual level. The emptiness you've experienced has been part of a necessary process; your spiritual taste test, if you will."

"What are You implying? That You sit by and watch while I uselessly try to make myself feel better?" Hurt laces my tone.

"First understand you won't be able to *fully* understand Me. That being said, I'll let you in on something you won't be thrilled to hear. During the time of Amos the prophet, the Israelites had distanced themselves from Me. Consequently, they went hungry in every city and 'lacked bread'[12] in every town in an effort to get them to return to Me."

My eyes widen. "So sometimes You *allow* unpleasant things, and other times You actually *cause* them?"

He takes both my hands into His huge ones, and looks me square in the eyes.

"I care about you. Make no mistake about that." He pauses. "But I know what's best for you, and it's not always what makes you happy. Will you accept good from Me and not trouble? There are things I wish to develop in you, things far richer and more vital than mere happiness. I want—no, I *need*—to be the one you find fulfillment in. The truth is, I am the *only* true and lasting source for fulfillment you'll find."

"Really?"

"Really." His gaze pierces my soul.

His voice takes on a lyrical quality as He says, "Come, everyone who thirsts, come to the waters; and he who has no money, come, buy and eat! Come, buy wine and milk without money and without price. Why do you spend your money for that which is not bread, and your labor for that which does not satisfy? Listen diligently to me, and eat what is good, and delight yourselves in rich food. Incline your ear, and come to me; hear, that your soul may live; and I will make with you an everlasting covenant, my steadfast, sure love for David."[13]

My brows knit together, an internal skirmish erupting in my mind. I bring my eyes back up to His. "My heart feels the truth of Your—" I search for the right word. "offer. But my head ... well, that's a different story."

"Your charred heart cannot be rebuilt with logic or even the most persuasive of arguments. I would know. I made it. And I'm the One who can fix it and fill it."

He puts my hands down, briefly touches my cheek, then walks over to our pile of gear. "Come help me set up our tents."

I oblige and grasp the slick material He hands me. We unfold it flat on the ground.

"Do you remember the burned-down house you saw during your drive out in the country?" He asks while unfurling the rods.

"You know about that too?"

"Of course!" He laughs. "How long has it been since you were last out there?"

"At least a year and a half." I say. "Why?"

"It's been re-built," He says with a gleam in His eye.

"I must admit," I say, "I did *not* see that coming. It seemed like it would remain a charred skeleton forever."

The Holy Spirit deftly locks the rods in place and begins to feed them into the corresponding tent flaps.

"You'd barely recognize the place. The only things that stayed the same are the circular driveway and brick work. It's a completely new floor plan." As He says this, the tent takes its full shape. He secures it to the ground and we move on to the second one.

We make quick work of tent number two and before I know it we're back at the fire.

"I work the same way you know," He says. "I can make all things new."

I begin nodding before I open my mouth to speak. "Yeah. I think I want You to go ahead and do that to my heart."

The Holy Spirit's smile is exultant. "You won't ever be sorry." He points to our gear and says, "Now, let Me make you dinner. I think you're *really* going to like it."

• Chapter 8 •
A Friendship Riddled With Paradox

Our gazes locked for a moment; his golden eyes were so deep that I imagined I could see all the way into his soul ... He looked back at me as if he could see my soul, too, and as if he liked what he saw.

Breaking Dawn, Stephenie Meyer[1]

One of my favorite pictures in the world is actually quite an awkward one. For starters, several of my husband's toes are visible in the background along with glimpses of his hairy legs draped over a chair right behind me. It's just a little out of place given the picture's subject. Another anomaly caught within the snapshot is my childhood teddy bear, clad in my homemade cape prototype, carelessly shoved into a face plant against my leg. And then there's the cameo made by my prominent nose as well as the part in my hair; my white scalp a stark contrast to the dark roots growing above my bottle-blond ends.

But none of those things were the focus of the picture. The reason the camera's shutter release button was depressed, making digital history, was to capture an embrace.

This photographic event took place during a family reunion of sorts. My brother Joe's brood was staying at our house when, one night, inevitably, bedtime for the kids arrived. My two nephews were ordered to give everyone good-night hugs. The youngest, Nathan (a.k.a. Nafey), who was almost two at the time, walked over to where I was kneeling and shocked me with a full-on hug.

It was a far cry from the shy, limp-noodle-lean-in I anticipated. He wrapped all thirty-one inches of his arm span around me and rested his small head on my shoulder. The hug took place over a long enough period of time for me to envelop his little frame in my arms and bury most of my face—prominent nose and all—in his shoulder. My aunt froze time with her Nikon, allowing me to re-live the occasion that showcased the crazy love that I feel toward not just one, but both nephews.

Sadly, those two boys did not always evoke such a deep emotional response from me. Geographically speaking, Jerimiah and I aren't close to either of our families. When my brother Joe's oldest son Luca was born, we were able to fly up to meet him a few days after his birth.

Nathan was born almost two years later. We lacked the funds to make that trip so I was reduced to meeting him through pictures. Time marched on as both boys grew and changed. Joe and my sister-in-law Amy relayed the boys' milestones to me as best they could over the phone. But I didn't ask much about them. Outside of the fact that we were related, I didn't even think about them a great deal. Appallingly, where my nephews were concerned, I was somewhat detached.

When Luca was a toddler and Nathan a rapidly evolving seven-month-old, Joe and Amy decided to fly down to Florida to visit my parents. Since Florida is within a reasonable driving distance for me, I invited myself down. Nothing could have prepared me for what happened next. My limited head knowledge about these two boys collided with my heart.

I knew Luca liked trucks and planes, but I had never before witnessed his face light up upon playing with them. I had seen Nafey's drooly smile in pictures, but had not yet known the joy of causing one. Have you ever tickled a child while they're standing up, only to scramble to catch them before they hit the floor because they're laughing so hard? I have. Little boy arms flung wide and heads pitched back with reckless abandon. Their shrieks of laughter hooked me like a narcotic. I never really stood a chance.

When it was time to leave, Mom and Dad drove my brother's family-of-four to the airport. I headed back to South Carolina at the same time. For a while, we drove side-by-side on the same stretch of four-lane highway. Then came their turnoff. I could barely make the road out through my tears as I waved goodbye. I am always sad to leave my family, but that departure was ten times worse. Those boys took with them a chunk of my heart.

Our visit together forever altered one thing. It was no longer possible for me to solely know *about* my nephews. Spending time with Luca and Nathan showed me that I want to *know* them.

I'm sure we're all aware that knowing *about* someone does not mean the same thing as *knowing* them. Facts only take you so far, which is one of the reasons I appreciate Edward Cullen's character so much.

In the first book, while he drove Bella to school and then back home again, he peppered her with questions. She was hyper-aware of how much she talked and felt certain she bored him. But she couldn't ignore the "absolute absorption of his face"[2] and the fact that his questions kept coming. So she answered, even when his questions made her responses more intricate.

Edward was after more than mere facts about Bella—birthday, favorite color, and if she ate SpaghettiOs as a kid. He sought the answers to her "whys." He wanted to know what she missed about the place she grew up, insisting on a description of anything he wasn't already aware of. He wanted to hear why she found the landscape there so beautiful. His business was about being schooled on the matters of her heart. He wanted to know her on a soul level.

What Edward sought with Bella is exactly what I dream of for my relationships. I'm not saying I'm a complicated person. I simply want to be understood. To be known. And who doesn't? I want those I care about most to get what makes me tick. I long for them to understand my humor, opinions and ideas, and to comprehend and at least appreciate what I hold dear.

My husband and I have this kind of relationship. Jerimiah understands me so well that it's sometimes easier for *him* to explain my thoughts to someone else. If you knew how often I get tongue-tied, you would know why this sometimes becomes necessary. And it's not just him. I also have several close girlfriends who are capable of playing a good game of Beth-Mad-Libs.

I am inserting a thoughtful pause here for dramatic effect.

Actual pause.

But no one cares about *all* the nuances of what I think, no matter how close we are. It is an unreal expectation for *any* relationship—even proud parents and happy marriages. Some of the things that go on in my head are simply too boring or convoluted for anyone else. I know this because *I've* been victimized by listening to my share of overly-detailed conversations. I may dearly love the person who is speaking, but my eyes glaze over upon hearing about the paper cut that sent them to Dr. Roundhouse at Chuck Norris Medical Group where they ran into Bessy Sue who gave them an amazing recipe for Spam Sushi and filled them in on the reason why Tad left the most horrible hand-model talent agency he ever had the misfortune to work for.

Of course, on the other hand, I would be in trouble if someone knew *all* the nuances of what I think. If someone could see through all my pretenses, like Michael Pardue saw through Delysia Lafosse's in the movie *Miss Pettigrew Lives*

For A Day, I might just come up short in the friend department.

Delysia Lafosse faced a bright, albeit complicated future. She was an American singer/actress living in London just before World War II ravaged Europe. She happened to be involved with three different men at the same time (and by involved, I mean sleeping with).

Phil was in charge of the play in which Delysia coveted the lead role. Nick owned the nightclub she performed in and also filled the role of her sugar daddy. Michael was a penniless pianist who was in love with her. Michael was also waiting for her response to his proposal of marriage.

But even with all she had going on, lie heaped upon lie, she appeared unfazed. She was high-spirited, charming, and flirtatious. She knew what she wanted in life and she was on the path to getting it. So if you strictly examined her from the outside, you'd never guess what was tumbling around inside her pretty little head:

> Delysia: (talking to the social-secretary-turned-friend she hired that very morning) Do you know what my name is, Guinevere?
> Guinevere: I was under the impression that it was Delysia Lafosse.
> Delysia: Sarah Grub. One of the Pittsburgh Grubs. My father is a steel worker. No one else in the world knows that apart from Michael. He doesn't judge me.
> Guinevere: No, he wouldn't.

Delysia: But you do.

Guinevere: *Me*? I certainly do not!

Delysia: Oh you think you don't but you do. This is all I own, Guinevere. And two dozen pairs of shoes. For all the fancy apartments and fashion shows, do you know how close I am to having nothing? Every day I wake up and I think, "If I make the wrong move, I could be out on that street with no clothes, no food, no job. And no friends. Just plain old Sarah Grub again." Do you know what that's like?[3]

Michael knew all about Phil and Nick and how Delysia was using each one. He knew what appearances she was struggling to keep up. He plain knew her.

I won't give away the ending for those of you who haven't seen it, but I can't help comparing myself to Delysia or, should I say, Sarah Grub. I, too, am often full of pretenses. No one, not even those who love me most in this world, knows who I am down deep.

But what if the last sentence is simply not true? What if someone exists who sees right through my pretense and *is* interested in my every thought? Someone whose eyes don't glaze over as I take an hour to awkwardly stutter over the details of my day, and knows I also choose to leave a few details out ...

O Lord, you have searched me and known me!
You know when I sit down and when I rise up; you discern my thoughts from afar.
You search out my path and my lying down and are acquainted with all my ways.
Even before a word is on my tongue, behold, O LORD, you know it altogether.
You hem me in, behind and before, and lay your hand upon me.
Such knowledge is too wonderful for me; it is high; I cannot attain it.
Where shall I go from your Spirit?
Or where shall I flee from your presence?
If I ascend to heaven, you are there!
If I make my bed in Sheol, you are there!
If I take the wings of the morning and dwell in the uttermost parts of the sea, even there your hand shall lead me, and your right hand shall hold me.
If I say, 'Surely the darkness shall cover me, and the light about me be night,' even the darkness is not dark to you; the night is bright as the day, for darkness is as light with you.
For you formed my inward parts; you knitted me together in my mother's womb.
I praise you, for I am fearfully and wonderfully made.

> Wonderful are your works; my soul knows it very well.
> My frame was not hidden from you, when I was being made in secret, intricately woven in the depths of the earth.
> Your eyes saw my unformed substance; in your book were written, every one of them, the days that were formed for me, when as yet there was none of them.
> How precious to me are your thoughts, O God!
> How vast is the sum of them!
> If I would count them, they are more than the sand.
> I awake, and I am still with you.
>
> Psalm 139:1-18[4]

From this passage, it's pretty clear God knows me even better than I know myself. He sees through the façades I carefully construct. He's aware of every trite thought making an appearance in my gray matter. The stunning part is, He seems to like me *in spite* of it all. I mean, I know He loves me, but it almost feels like He would enjoy sitting down with me over a cup of coffee. Like what friends do. How could I feel anything but cherished by this revelation?

Genesis 1:27 says, "So God created man in his own image, in the image of God he created him; male and female he created them."[5] If it's true, then I can actually draw information about God simply from the way I'm wired.

And if I desire to be known for who I really am *so* desperately, am I crazy to believe *He* desires to be known in a similar fashion? To be understood, at least in some part? That I would come to know what makes *Him* tick? Grow to understand *His* humor? Take the time to comprehend and appreciate what *He* holds dear? Maybe He implanted that need deep in my heart so I would one day recognize it's a reflection of His own desire.

> God formed us for His pleasure, and so formed us that we as well as He, can in divine communion enjoy the sweet and mysterious mingling of kindred personalities. He meant us to see Him and live with Him and draw our life from His smile.
>
> *The Pursuit Of God*, A.W. Tozer[6]

But is it truly possible to know God? Or at least *get to know* Him? I mean, look at the overarching picture of God. He's immeasurable—a fact that has long driven me to view Him as untouchable and distant, even aloof. However, as we're all aware, knowing information *about* an individual is not equal to actually *knowing them.*

1 Corinthians 2:10-12 would indicate knowing God *is* possible for followers of Christ because of the Holy Spirit. "These things God has revealed to us through the Spirit. For the Spirit searches everything, even the depths of God. For who knows a person's thoughts except the spirit of that

person, which is in him? So also no one comprehends the thoughts of God except the Spirit of God. Now we have received not the spirit of the world, but the Spirit who is from God, that we might understand the things freely given us by God."[7]

Okay, I get it. It *is* possible and God desires it. But what does "knowing" Him look like on a practical level?

I am the happy wearer of contact lenses. While I've grown out of the plastic purple frames I had in fourth grade, I still don't like the way glasses look on me. They are also horrible to wear while exercising, especially if you sweat as profusely as I do.

One steamy September night a few years ago, I wanted to run laps in my neighborhood with my dog/jogging partner Daisy. This occurred on the same day my eyes refused entry of my contacts and I was forced into spec-dom. I decided to run anyway. The first three laps were interesting.

Lap one: Perpetual bouncing/shimmying of frames. Onset of mild motion sickness.

Lap two: Add fogged up lenses to lap one and repeat (several attempts to wipe them using non-sweaty t-shirt parts failed miserably).

Lap three: Disheartened halt in the driveway while contemplating options; meanwhile, my jogging partner runs around the front yard sniffing for and eating feral cat poop (one of her favorite snacks).

My choices were pitiful. If I continued on bespectacled, I was quite sure motion-sickness-induced-vomiting would be somewhere in my near future. I could instead admit defeat and tuck tail inside. *Or,* I could run without my glasses. Blind as a bat.

Without further deliberation, I reached up, pulled off my glasses, and folded them neatly on the hood of my car. Smart move or not, I popped in both headphones and Daisy and I took off into the darkness.

It was terrifying. I was enshrouded in shadow and would not even be able to hear danger approach. Because of my poor vision, all I could make out were distant luminous orbs and house blobs. I suppressed several screams, mistaking a mailbox for a person creeping up on me.

But, before I knew what was happening, my apprehension bloomed into exhilaration. The vague lights became beautiful shimmers enhancing the soft night. The music pulsing in my ears was crisp and clear, my own private concert. I didn't have to remind my legs to lengthen their stride because they did it of their own accord (in fact, the rest of my body almost had to catch up). I felt alive. And I must say I had never before lost myself so fully in the chore of exercise.

Later, after I was safely indoors, I ruminated on my new-found ability to run blind. How had I been able to do it? The more I thought, the more I remembered just how many laps I'd actually taken around my 'hood prior to that evening.

I'd spent countless hours jogging or walking around the same half-mile loop; getting to know every dip, turn, and pothole in the pavement. It turns out I knew my neighborhood like Daisy knows the smell of cat poop. Though I would never have known it if I hadn't been forced to give up the senses I'd most always relied on, not to mention the ones that made the most sense. I wouldn't have been able to shift my focus onto what turned out to be one of the more freeing and memorable experiences of my life.

So how does my relationship with God relate to my little adventure? Similar to the streets in my neighborhood, I've put in a lot of time with God throughout the years. Maybe even enough to recognize His voice. But I don't think I will really get to know Him until I'm able to remove my "spiritual glasses" and run blind with Him.

The "spiritual glasses" represent all the facts I've compiled in order to give me clarity about this Divine Being known as God. Facts are a foundation, of course, but have a tendency of becoming foggy and getting displaced easily. Facts without experience have distorted my relationship with God. They have quite possibly even induced spiritual sickness. I have a feeling there's a lot I've been missing by keeping my spiritual spectacles on.

> We are placed on this planet to enjoy the greatness of God and to declare His greatness as greater than all the evils within human hearts. By entering His presence and enjoying His friendship, we begin to truly love Him ...

Dr. L. Douglas Dorman,
Your Next Step Ministries[8]

• • •

Night is in full swing around our campsite. The velvety sky is the backdrop for hundreds of gleaming stars which seem close enough to touch. With my stomach satisfied, I sprawl across the opening of my tent and pop my head out to talk. The Holy Spirit reclines a few feet away, leaning His back against a smooth rock.

With no other human around to help carry the chit-chat, a heavy and somewhat awkward silence creeps in unawares.

The Holy Spirit breaks the pregnant pause. "Have you ever—in your life—had a friend who did all the talking? About themselves, I mean?"

Relieved by His new topic lifeline, I answer with a loud "Ha! Have I ever! Talk about annoying." I muse silently for a moment and then pipe back up.

"Come to think of it, I guess I wouldn't really classify the self-talker as a friend. More of an acquaintance to avoid unless I have the time and patience to listen."

He cocks His head and stares curiously at me. "So how would you define friendship?"

My response is swift. "Waaay more of give-and-take. Equal parts talking *and* listening. Asking questions in order to understand the other person and prove you really care." I hesitate and narrow my eyes thoughtfully. "Being interested in what's going on with them. So much so that you can laugh with them when they laugh and cry with them when their heart breaks. To me, that's a true friend."

His expression gives nothing away as He asks, "How would you rate *yourself* as a friend?"

I eye Him cautiously and wonder if it's a trick question.

He flashes me a brief smile then opens His mouth and begins a song, revealing a rich, baritone voice.

"We could talk for hours
It doesn't matter
You don't hear a word I say
'Cause you don't listen when I speak
So I'll sing instead

La la la la la I love you
Ooh I really do
If you ever paid attention
I think you would love Me too

You say you want to know Me
I get the feeling that you're telling me a lie
'Cause every time I talk about emotion
You shake your pretty head and say goodbye

La la la la la I love you
Ooh I really do
If you ever paid attention
I think you would love Me too

Why do I love you like I do
When you ignore Me
Just like the sun ignores the moon
All you see is you

I love you
Ooh sad but true
If you ever paid attention
I think you would love Me too"[9]

The last note fades and He says, "My girl JJ Heller wrote that. What do you think?"

My eyes are frozen as saucers, not only because He just sang so well, but also at the song's implication. "Exactly what are you saying?"

He looks thoughtful for a moment and then responds. "I know you'll always have needs, and I want you to come to Me for everything. You were, after all, created to need Me. But I want you to go beyond that. I want your friendship—the *real* friendship you just described."

I come to a sitting position and wrap my arms around my legs. "I—I've never really thought about being *friends* with You before," I stutter. "Isn't that sort of a paradox? A pathetic human creation becoming friends with her—" I eye Him warily "—divine Creator?"

His voice is soft. "Why do you think Jesus died on the cross for you and then gave you the gift of My presence?"

"To save humanity from an eternity of separation from Him." I huff mildly. "But that's not the same thing as *friendship.*"

"Stop focusing on the grand narrative. We both know I don't want your life to be all about you and your desires, but at some point you've got to realize just how personal our relationship is designed to be," He says.

I look down at my knees. "I feel like I should only be talking to You about the important stuff: sins, confession, big life decisions that will help point people to You. And those are not the normal conversations I have with friends." I hesitate. "At least the first two aren't."

"Well I *do* want you to talk to Me about the important stuff. As well as all the rest. Even the things you feel are stupid." He leans over and tilts my chin up to look at Him. "Quit editing when you talk to Me—I already know anyway. Our friendship will only grow as soon as you drop the pretenses and get real."

A question bothers me as I stare at Him. "But didn't You just point out that I'm always talking about myself?"

He laughs softly. "I did. You've got to take your own advice and listen to what *I* have to say too." He pauses. "It's more than that though." I see a shadow of grief in His eyes.

"I want you to ask questions and be interested in what's going on with Me. I want you to care about what makes Me laugh and the things that break My heart."

I'm overwhelmed with guilt for long moments.

"I hear what You're saying." I drop my eyes again and pull at imaginary fuzz on my sleeve. "I don't really pay attention to You until I need something. And that's not being a friend."

I bring my eyes up to His and say slowly, "But I don't know how to relate to You in the current world. I mean, the only context I have of You is from writings of bygone days." I struggle to put my thoughts into words. "I know You're not stuck in a biblical timeline, but I can't seem to view You in any other way," I admit, feeling helpless.

"I know," He says with a slow smile. "I've got just the thing that will help." A subtle hint of excitement laces His tone.

I just stare at Him.

The Holy Spirit reaches into His gargantuan pack and pulls out an electronic contraption. He sets it on top of a tall boulder and fiddles with it for a few seconds.

I hear the first few bars of music and am surprised by the volume and bass produced by the lone device. But that is not what sends my jaw flapping downward.

The song I hear is instantly recognizable. It's the mixture of hip hop, jazz, and funk swirled together in a ballad so hauntingly optimistic that people in distress hear it and laugh in the face of their evil tormentors—otherwise known as *Ikes Mood I.*

And the Holy Spirit is dancing to it. I can't tear my eyes away. He's got moves like I've never seen.

"What in the holy swagger is going on right now?" I holler over the song.

His moves don't falter as He exclaims, "I know, right?"

Smooth and effortless, His body defies gravity. The beat continues to thump as I watch Him Hustle, Jerk, Moonwalk, and a plethora of other moves that probably haven't even been dreamed up. The campfire only emphasizes the impressive display as His shadow leaps and undulates against the inky backdrop.

While I sit and look on in awe my head bobs with the music and my feet tap in rhythm; my body is all but dancing. I feel pure joy course through my veins as I watch this impressive display. I laugh in delight and cry over His sheer wonder all at the same time. I've seen nothing like it in all my life.

As the song dies and another fills the airwaves, the Holy Spirit makes His way over to me with a gleam in His eye. He pauses and extends both hands down to me in an unspoken offer.

"Are You kidding me?" I shake my head violently. "I can't dance!"

He ignores my protests and pulls me to my feet to show me some dance steps. Unfortunately, I am like a fawn discovering her legs. But He is a patient teacher. He gives instruction over the ruckus of the music, and we both crack up at my two left feet.

The genres of music change constantly; the songs are seemingly every flavor under the sun. Jazz, bluegrass, funk, epic film scores, dubstep, Celtic, hip-hop ...

Pretty soon, I've all but forgotten about my gawky moves and shed my inhibitions. I am dancing next to Him with all my might and loving every second. He picks me up and swings me high above His head, letting go then grabbing me again on my way back down. My breath catches in my throat, but the second time He tosses me I am ready. During my freefall, I splay my arms wide and throw my head back—bursting with the joy that is His presence.

We continue on for some time before the Holy Spirit turns the music down and puts a hand on my shoulder to still me and suggest a break.

I take long, greedy gulps of water as my breathing slows. I shake my head in amazement.

"I had no idea You were into those kinds of music! I always took You for an organ/choir aficionado." I speak so quickly my words practically fall all over each other. "And Your moves—don't even get me started! You're ah-mazing!"

"This is only the beginning," He says with a radiant smile. "Do you understand yet? You're my friend when you spend time with Me; not simply for what I do for you, but because You enjoy My presence. And My presence is enjoyable."

I blink in wonder and a huge grin splits my face. "Yes. Yes, I think I'm finally starting to see that."

I casually toss my empty water container in my tent and then walk to the boulder where the music contraption sits. I look over at the Holy Spirit with eyebrows arched in question. At His approving nod, I crank up the volume once more. We resume our revelry as the moon creeps higher in the night sky.

• Chapter 9 •
The Great Expansive Somewhere

She had always suffered from a vague restlessness, a longing for adventure that she told herself severely was the result of reading too many novels when she was a small child. As she grew up, and particularly after her mother died, she had learned to ignore that restlessness. She had nearly forgotten about it, till now.

The Blue Sword, Robin McKinley[1]

It all started with a particularly interesting church bulletin issued one fateful Sunday morning. On the cover, the little girl was kneeling next to her bed, hands clasped together in prayer. She had a solemn face and a smooth mullet, as if her mother had recently combed out her mane in a nighttime ritual.

To say that my thirteen-year-old self and best friend Julie found the image amusing would be a gross understatement. Rather than listen to the drone of the sermon, we crafted mutton chops onto mullet-girl's profile and drew thought bubbles out to the side—filling them with imaginary prayers about unicorns and bodily functions.

It did not take long for our hushed giggling to escalate. Soon, our lips clamped shut, tears of laughter streamed out of our squinted eyes, and the whole pew began to rattle as our shoulders heaved with violent shaking. Our antics eventually went so far as to earn us the stank-eye from our perturbed pastor.

This was not an isolated incident. It happened so frequently during my growing-up years I gave it a title: Church Pew Hysterics (CPH for short). The CPH took place because I was bored. B-o-r-e-d. And I blamed my boredom solely on church. For good reason, too.

I was there the majority of the day every Sunday. My only reprieve was a few hours in the afternoon for Mom's pot roast and a fleeting nap before returning to the brick prison to attend the dreaded nighttime service. Most Wednesdays I had to walk over to church after school, leaving me with hours to kill while waiting for the scheduled evening programs to begin.

I was there *so* often, and it was *so* uninteresting I was practically *forced* to come up with my own means of entertainment. For example, a friend and I discovered a way, using a half-wall here and an awning there, to climb onto the roof of the church. We would crouch behind A.C. units to watch the traffic whiz by, all the while discussing aspects of high-school drama. And when herded into the sanctuary, my friends and I clamored for a seat in the balcony. It was the perfect location for counting chandeliers, farting powerfully enough to vibrate a pew, and throwing spitballs into the bouffants of the unfortunate, more seasoned souls sitting below.

Needless to say, I was hopeful the adult world did not contain this high a concentration of boredom. I just *knew* as soon as I was free from the adolescent curse of being dragged to church nearly every time the doors were open, my boredom would pass.

Fast forward into my early thirties. Sometimes I catch myself singing a song—out of the blue—I'm *positive* I did not recently hear on the radio or television. Song lyrics are subconsciously triggered by certain words, I think.

Here's an example: Let's say that "small" and "world" are thought within rapid succession of each other. I will soon be humming the repetitious song overheard on Disney's "it's a small world" ride. (I have long believed this song may, in fact, be a viable method of torture to extract information from members of al-Qaeda.)

The random singing is not a new phenomenon to me. And I don't usually evaluate the steps it took for my mind to activate the phantom melodies. However, one song I all-too-recently found myself belting out *did* make me pause. It was Belle's musings from *Beauty and The Beast*. She sang about adventure and wanting more than the life she was currently living. She wanted a far greater experience than what society had planned for her.

Where in the world did *that* song come from? I stopped, reflected, and realized I was caught up in the daily grind of the adult world. Earn money, spend money, cook, clean, eat, shower, dress, attend weddings, pay taxes, exercise, watch TV, get haircut, file fingernails, go to birthday parties, do laundry, grocery shop, etc.

Life.

So monotonous.

I could no longer point the finger at my religious yesteryear. I was all grown up and *still* existing in a state of boredom. The truth is, you don't escape boredom just because you grow up. You're either too busy to notice or simply forced to stop whining about it because you have no one to blame but yourself.

By boredom, I mean that nagging, restless feeling, in which contentment is ultimately elusive. You feel the incessant urge to think something, to do something, to *be* something you're not. But you don't even know what that something is.

Enter ennui.

Ennui (ahn-**wee**) means a feeling of utter weariness and discontent resulting from satiety or lack of interest.[2] I thought I understood the word satiety in context, but decided to look it up anyway. Satiety means the state of being fed or gratified *to or beyond* capacity.[3]

Meaning, the awful plight of boredom is caused by either a complete lack of interest *or* absolute excess. This leads me to believe ennui could be the motive behind at least half of all mid-life crises, drunken bar fights, affairs, poofy 80's bangs, and a slew of other morally reprehensible behaviors.

What's that you say? I experience ennui because my heart secretly longs for the *adventure* Belle sings about? Oh.

My. Gosh. How utterly Disney-esque and lame. Admitting that makes me feel hokey because adventure is a goofy word in today's society. It's awkward. *I* can't even take the word seriously. It's a term seemingly reserved for children's books and the eccentric folk who eat, sleep, and breathe renaissance fairs.

On the other hand, I *am* a hopeless romantic. And a romantic defined is a person dominated by idealism, *a desire for adventure*, chivalry, etc.[4] So, it sort of makes sense.

But what is adventure anyway? Ask two different people and you're sure to get two different answers. At first glance, even the dictionary seems a bit confused. There are two somewhat different definitions given on Dictionary.com:

> 1. Participation in an exciting or very unusual experience (This definition makes me think of taking children to the circus.)
> 2. A bold, usually risky undertaking; hazardous action of uncertain outcome (While this definition has me thinking of passion, swordfights, and daring rescue.)[5]

Only when I examine the word "exciting"—found in definition #1—do the two separate definitions begin to solidify a bit more. Excitement does not always result in squeals of delighted laughter from children as I once assumed (based on the *typical* usage of the word). To "excite" is actually to awaken, stir up, or provoke.[6]

With all that being said, I came up with the Beth-translation of adventure: Provocation into a dangerous endeavor of unknown consequence.

This gives adventure a more serious meaning than I originally thought. My re-write almost makes adventure sound ... epic. Like being part of something bigger than myself; something outside of my own private gain. The interpretation of adventure suggests my possible engagement in a story that *actually* matters in the grand scheme of life.

Nice. I'm feeling slightly less Disney-esque and lame.

Is it possible I could learn a thing or two from characters in adventures and epic tales? Maybe. I think, much like me, they are often unremarkable. At least they start out that way. But, whether they realize it or not, somewhere on their journey these characters find themselves drawn to a task only they specifically can carry out. Drawn? Called? Chosen? Who knows the best way to phrase it? I think Katniss Everdeen from the *Hunger Games* trilogy captured what I'm trying to say during a monologue in the last book.

> I begin to fully understand the lengths to which people have gone to protect me. What I mean to the rebels. My ongoing struggle against the Capitol, which has so often felt like a solitary journey, has not been undertaken alone. I have thousands upon thousands of people from the districts at my side. *I was their Mockingjay long before I accepted the role.*

Mockingjay, Suzanne Collins[7]

You see, Katniss never signed up to become the symbol of freedom for her country of Panem. Yet she was drawn into an adventure impacting more than just her and those she loved. She was forced to throw caution and fear to the side and step into the business meant for her. Two famous characters from *The Lord of the Rings* also experienced a powerful pull and were faced with a similar consequential decision:

> "I don't like anything here at all," said Frodo, "step or stone, breath or bone. Earth, air and water all seem accursed. But so our path is laid." "Yes, that's so," said Sam. "And we shouldn't be here at all, if we'd known more about it before we started. But I suppose it's often that way. The brave things in the old tales and songs, Mr. Frodo: adventures, as I used to call them. I used to think that they were things the wonderful folk of the stories went out and looked for, because they wanted them, because they were exciting and life was a bit dull, a kind of a sport, as you might say. But that's not the way of it with the tales that really mattered, or the ones that stay in the mind. Folk seem to have been just landed in them, usually—their paths were laid that way, as you put it. But I expect

> they had lots of chances, like us, of turning back, only they didn't. And if they had, we shouldn't know, because they'd have been forgotten."
>
> *The Lord of The Rings, The Two Towers,*
> J.R.R. Tolkien[8]

Most readers know the ending to Frodo and Samwise Gamgee's tale. But I'd like to focus on the beginning—for it answers the question of all questions regarding stories of epic proportion. Where exactly does one find adventure of great

consequence? The kind that sucker punches ennui in the gut?

Adventure is apparently impossible to pinpoint. I mean, why else would Belle be singing about the great expansive *somewhere*? Frodo didn't know he would have a story when he first laid eyes on his Uncle Bilbo's ring. He certainly wasn't looking for one. Samwise Gamgee likewise had no clue of the journey his innocent eavesdropping would land him in. Yet they found themselves thrust into the heart of an epic story, one that was pivotal to the survival of all inhabiting Middle Earth. And so the truth became clear to me:

You don't *find* adventure of great consequence. Real adventure finds *you*.

• • •

A deep, rich voice drifts into my consciousness in mid-song. Blinking against intense rays of sunlight, I peer through my sleepy lids and sit up slowly. It's morning at our camp and the Holy Spirit is singing and cooking what smells like breakfast.

I must have fallen asleep with my torso facing the fire and my legs tucked into the sleeping bag under the canopy of my tent. Feeling something soft where my head was resting, I look down and notice my travel companion put His sleeping bag under my head as a pillow at some point during the night.

The realization brings a sweet smile to my face, which is overrun by a noisy yawn and a stretch.

"Morning," the Holy Spirit calls, breaking His song.

"Hi," I say, my voice scratchy from lack of use.

"How about some food and then we'll head out?"

"Sounds good."

Stiffly, I stumble onto my feet and make my way toward the privacy of the boulders. After a few minutes, I come back to camp, eat and then help the Holy Spirit put everything back into His gargantuan pack.

We gear up, attach our lines, and head down the rock face once more. The Holy Spirit and I fall into a matching rhythm of skimming the air and slow descent. He doesn't seem to be in any particular hurry. Thoughts swarm and I am lost in their thickness for a time. A huge sigh escapes my lungs, echoing the activity in my brain.

He turns His head to look at me. "What are you thinking about?"

I glance at Him, dismayed. "Something is ... off with me right now. I feel restless and discontent. But I can't quite put my finger on the problem. It's depressing, you know?" My tone is sour.

"Yes, I know."

My face scrunches up in confusion. "It depresses You too?"

"No—that's not quite what I meant," He answers with a chuckle. "But you're accurate when you say something is off."

My smile feels thin. "Oh ... right." I sigh again, this time with a more dramatic flare. "What can be done?"

"Are you sure you want to hear?" He asks.

I stare at Him. "I was sort of asking that question rhetorically."

He shoots me a knowing look. "That's an understatement—it wasn't a question, it was bad acting."

"Okay ... maybe I was being a *tad* melodramatic." I flash a sheepish smile. "Go ahead. I'm listening."

"There's something I want you to do."

My shoulders slump slightly. "Pul-ease don't tell me You want me to read some *lame* self-help book."

He ignores my statement. "I want you to quit your job."

My feet grind to a halt on the slippery rock. Mouth turned downward, I blink rapidly in confusion over the implications of being jobless. "Say what?"

The Holy Spirit continues down past me at a smooth pace. "You heard me right. Quit your job as a Realtor and write about your time with Me."

"Hold up. You don't want me to *read* a lame self-help book. You want me to *write* one?"

He has to tilt His head back and look up to see me now. "Not self-help," He calls. "Our *experience* together."

I huff and then scramble to close the gap between us. There is a long silence as we continue down together at the same pace.

"You're crazy." I pause again. "And mean. You know how I dislike being in sales so why would You tease me this way?"

"I'm not joking."

"If You're not messing with me, then how in the world are Jerimiah and I supposed to survive without my income? We're barely making it as is."

"And the word of the LORD came to him (Elijah): 'Depart from here and turn eastward and hide yourself by the brook Cherith, which is east of the Jordan. You shall drink from the brook, and I have commanded the ravens to feed you there.' So he went and did according to the word of the LORD. He went and lived by the brook Cherith that is east of the Jordan. And the ravens brought him bread and meat in the morning, and bread and meat in the evening, and he drank from the brook."[9]

I arch an eyebrow. "You're planning on sending ravens with a check to cover our mortgage?"

His deep laugh is quick to follow. "What you need will be provided for."

"Well I need a place to live!" I retort. "Preferably in the house I've got." My face falls into a pout. "I really like the hardwood floors. Plus we finally painted colors we like." The last words of my sentence come out in a pathetic mutter.

The Holy Spirit inhales. Exhales. "You are going to have to satisfy yourself with the knowledge that I will take care of you in the way *I* see fit."

"Oh, that's just great!" My free hand flies up in outrage. "So what You're asking me to do is willingly stand to the side and watch while everything I hold dear is stripped from me. You apparently want us to become destitute. Thanks for the great life plan." The last several words drip with sarcastic hostility.

"You assume too much."

"Well *You* aren't telling me enough!"

His tone is resolute. "And I never will. Get used to it."

My mouth gapes open in shock.

"And without faith it is impossible to please him, for whoever would draw near to God must believe that he exists and that he rewards those who seek him,"[10] He quotes.

My brain scrambles for new excuses. "W-Well Jerimiah will never go for it."

Suddenly, I come up with an even better argument. "Plus, I *read* books. I don't write them. Passing high school English does *not* qualify me to become a writer." I smile triumphantly; positive I have Him with that one.

"You let Me handle Jerimiah. And look at it this way, *I'm* the author and *you* are My pen of choice—or typist in this case."

I let it sink in. I visualize people laughing at what I have to say or, even worse, ignoring it all together. "Why would You do this to me?" I moan woefully.

He looks at me, disappointment evident in His gaze. "You're being typically self-centered. Especially considering how much is at stake."

"What in the world are You talking about?"

It takes me a moment to realize He's come to an abrupt stop. My feet slide to a halt just below Him.

He walks Himself down to my side and says in a thick voice, "The world *is* what I'm talking about."

Our heads swivel toward each other as we lean back slightly in our harnesses to perch over nothingness. I eye Him and wait for His explanation.

"Do you realize that the souls of humanity hang in the balance? On an ongoing basis? 'And he (Jesus) died for all, that those who live might no longer live for themselves but for him who for their sake died and was raised.'[11] Do you really think your life—your existence—is about *you*?"

I shake my head. "No," I say quickly. "I-I mean sometimes," I admit grudgingly. "But I know it really isn't supposed to be."

"Do you even begin to comprehend the chasm that exists between Me and those who don't know and accept what Jesus did on the cross? The peril of their position? It's not merely a physical death I'm referring to. Heaven is real, but so is hell. Those who don't belong to Jesus when they die will suffer a second death—a spiritual death—and an eternity of torment and separation from the Father. Much of the world is in dire straits."

Tears prick at my conscience as I listen in silence.

"I didn't call you to a life of playing it safe or even one of relative comfort. I called you to a life of obedience—to tell other people about Me and My love for them. I want the same closeness with each one of them that we share." He pauses. "Do you think it's accidental that I'm telling you to do this scary thing at the same time you feel so restless and discontent; so bored?" He shakes His head.

"I've been prepping you for the part you're to play in humanity's story. You have an adventure in which to engage."

"Adventure?" I puzzle over His word choice.

"Yes, adventure. Unfortunately, adventures rarely look appealing to those with a role to play in them. Spectators are far more likely to romanticize it than those involved because spectators are not the ones being sifted and refined."

I stare at Him. "What are You saying?"

"Adventures are actually difficult undertakings. They come with a price."

"Ugh." My eyes briefly slide shut and then re-open.

His face bares the hint of a smile. "Let me explain what I mean."

"Please do." My eyebrows rise expectantly.

He pushes off the wall and descends again. I quickly fall in sync.

"In the days of the Persian empire, there was a beautiful woman named Esther. Because of an edict from the king, she was torn from her family and brought to his palace along with many other virginal beauties in an effort to find a replacement queen."

"Replacement?"

"The former one, Vashti, ticked the king off and was therefore banned from his presence. Not much new there." He smiles. "Vying to become the new queen, each girl would undergo a year of beauty treatments before she was allowed her night spent with the king."

I suddenly laugh. “Dang. That would've made for some *good* television—like the ultimate season of *The Bachelor*. Large gathering of competitive and conniving estrogen—check. One man being fawned over—check. Marriage proposal at stake—check.”

“We’re talking about virgins here,” He comments dryly.

My brows practically shoot up to my hairline in surprise as I wonder if He really just said what I think He did.

“Anyway,” He continues, “after her twelve months of spiffing up, Esther was taken in to the king. ‘The king loved Esther more than all the women, and she won grace and favor in his sight more than all the virgins, so that he set the royal crown on her head and made her queen instead of Vashti.’”[12]

I wait for Him to continue, but He remains silent. “Well ... how *exactly* was a year of beauty treatment a difficult undertaking? It’s not like they had chemical peels or electrolysis back then. And don't get me wrong—her situation didn’t start out as ideal—but she became *queen* for crying out loud. She pretty much hit the mother lode.”

“She had a secret,” the Holy Spirit says.

“Ooh. A little intrigue. *Now* it’s getting good.”

“Her *real* name was Hadassah, and she was Jewish—a fact that her guardian Mordecai forbade her to reveal to anyone. And it ended up being a good thing he did.”

“Why? The king didn't like Jews?” I speculate.

“No, the king wasn’t the problem. His highest official Haman was.”

“So *Haman* didn’t like Jews.”

"He didn't have a problem with them unless they refused to pay him honor like Esther's uncle Mordecai did. You could say Haman was on a bit of a power trip."

"Lemme guess. Mordecai spit in Haman's face."

"Nope. He only refused to kneel before Haman, which made Haman see red," He says.

"Haman had some definite anger issues," I comment.

"That's a bit of an understatement. The idea of killing Mordecai as punishment wasn't enough for him. Once Haman found out Mordecai was Jewish, he decided to have every last Jew in the Persian Empire murdered."

"Whoa. Overkill!" I cringe at my accidental pun. "Haman must've had some serious power to pull those kinds of strings."

"He sort of tricked the king into believing the Jews were an unmanageable and disobedient people needing to be destroyed, even though they were nothing of the sort. His plan was soon put into motion. 'Letters were sent by couriers to all the king's provinces with instruction to destroy, to kill, and to annihilate all Jews, young and old, women and children, in one day, the thirteenth day of the twelfth month, which is the month of Adar, and to plunder their goods. A copy of the document was to be issued as a decree in every province by proclamation to all the peoples to be ready for that day.'"[13]

"That's horrible!" One foot stumbles as I land on an uneven patch of rock. I right myself and continue down.

"It was," He says. "As you could imagine, Mordecai and all the Jews living in the capital were pretty despondent about their impending death."

I am a tad bewildered. "What about Esther?"

"She didn't hear of it at first."

"How is *that* possible? She was the *queen*."

"Yes, but she wasn't privy to all the king's decrees or even his thoughts. And she was sequestered in palace life, so it's not surprising the only way she found out was through her secret meetings with Mordecai. He told her to 'go to the king to beg his favor and plead with him on behalf of her people.'"[14]

I look at the Holy Spirit and say, "That's a no-brainer. Of course she should've done that."

Out of the corner of my eye, I see Him shaking his head even before I'm done talking. "You're not thinking clearly. She lived in a much different time than you."

"Explain, please."

"Esther told Mordecai, 'All the king's servants and the people of the king's provinces know that if any man or woman goes to the king inside the inner court *without* being called, there is but one law—*to be put to death*, except the one to whom the king holds out the golden scepter so that he may live. But as for me, I have not been called to come in to the king these thirty days.'"[15]

"Oh, I see," I say. "Not the best position to be in."

"Exactly."

"What did Mordecai say to her?" I ask.

"Do not think to yourself that in the king's palace you will escape any more than all the other Jews. For if you keep silent at this time, relief and deliverance will rise for the Jews from another place, but you and your father's house will perish. And who knows whether you have not come to the kingdom for such a time as this?"[16]

"Fairly compelling argument," I say, mostly to myself. "Did she agree to it?" I ask Him.

The Holy Spirit nods. "She sent a reply to Mordecai asking him to gather all the Jews living in the capital city and fast three days for her. She agreed to do the same and said, 'Then I will go to the king, though it is against the law, and if I perish, I perish.'"[17]

"Wow," I say after a moment. "That's pretty heavy."

"No kidding." He pauses.

"So, do you think at any point in time Esther was like—" He raises His voice an octave to sound mockingly feminine and flutters a hand to His chest. 'Oh just look at the *adventure* I'm about to go on! I can't wait to face certain death in order to save my people! Yay!'" He puts His free hand on His cheek with exaggerated enthusiasm.

I laugh at His impersonation. "No," I say between chuckles. "Not really."

"That's the thing about adventures," the Holy Spirit says. "Esther had no guarantees about the outcome of her actions. And it was not a position she signed up for. But she knew far more was at stake than her own life or well-being. So she stepped into the business meant for her." His eyes find mine. "Are you willing to do the same?"

My breath catches in my throat and I look at Him with a nervous smile. Finding myself at a loss for words, I nod instead.

"Good," He says. "Esther lived *and* saved her people from annihilation, but you may not always see the full outcome of your adventures."

I frown at this.

"*But*," He pauses, "I guarantee you're pleasing me when you do what I ask of you. I won't ever leave you. I won't ever forsake you. And I *will* give you what you need to carry out each adventure."

His promises seem to wrap around me, calming my nerves. We descend in silence.

We draw closer to the ground with each passing minute. I can now make out thick clusters of trees bordered by a shimmering river cutting through a wide valley. A short time later, our feet touch the rich soil blanketing the edge of the forest floor.

"We made it!" I say with a huge smile. But my face falls slowly.

Noticing my look, the Holy Spirit tilts my chin up as His brow furrows. "What is it?" He asks.

"We made it," I say again flatly. "End of story."

He wraps me in His strong embrace and kisses the top of my head. I feel Him sigh contentedly. After He releases me, He moves to deftly disconnect us from the ropes and harnesses.

"You're wrong, you know."

"How?" I ask. "I followed the sign at the top of this mountain. The arrow pointed down. And now we're here at the bottom."

His laugh catches me off guard. "Silly Beth! Loving Me

isn't an achievement. It's a life-long journey." He points behind me, toward the thick canopy of the forest.

I whirl around to look. I see nothing but rich hues of green and brown for a moment. Then I gasp and race to the tree line.

My fingers trace the familiar words "To Love God" on the rough, wooden sign. There is a faint path heading straight under the lush forest cover. The realization the Holy Spirit and I don't have to part ways hits me, and tears of joy begin to trickle down my face.

Moments later, the Holy Spirit arrives at my side, fresh gear strapped to His back. He offers His hand and I place mine into his firm grasp.

"Shall we continue on?" He asks with a smile.

Beaming, I nod. Hand-in-hand, we follow the narrow pathway in the direction of the sign's arrow and begin the next part of our adventure.

• May I have a word with you? •

Thank you so much for taking the time to read my story. Now that you've read it, you are—by default—my friend. The only way to break this bond is to either eat copious amounts of liver pate while blowing the stench in my face or to throw me a Pennywise-themed birthday party. (And I still might forgive you for the liver-breath-blowing.) Believe me or not, I care about you and would really enjoy meeting you in some way, shape, or form.

If you don't yet have a relationship with Jesus Christ, I hope this book makes you want to experience your own love story with Him. If you already do, I hope you're encouraged and emboldened to fall even more deeply in love with Him—no matter what shape your journey takes. But at the very least, I hope you were entertained and got in a good laugh or two.

If you like my story, here are some ways you can help:

1. Give *Let Me Fall* a review on Amazon. I can't stress how important this is or how much it will help me. You can review the book on Amazon even if you didn't purchase it from there. Simply create an account (if you don't already have one) and log in. Look up *Let Me Fall*, and once you're on the product page, scroll to the bottom and click on the link that reads: Write a customer review. It's that simple.

2. Ask your friends, family, doctor, accountant, pool-repair man, gardener, boss, bodyguards, and personal chef to buy a copy. If you do this, I am in your debt.

3. Stay connected with me through the following:
www.bethpensinger.com or www.letmefall.me
Follow me on twitter: @bethpensinger
Like my Facebook author page:
www.facebook.com/BethPensinger
Follow me on Pinterest: Beth Pensinger
Follow me on Instagram: @bpruwithme

A simple "thank you" is not enough, but it is all I have. Thank you friend.

Yours,
Beth

• Notes •

Preface

1. Tozer, A.W. *The Pursuit of God*. 1948. Project Gutenberg(EBook #25141).

2. Robinson, Robert. "Come Thou Fount of Every Blessing." Split Infinity Music. Worship LIVE! Accessed February 11, 2013. http://www.simusic.com/worship/hymns/.

Chapter 1

1. Philippians 4:8, ESV

Chapter 2

1. Matthew 26:74-75, ESV

2. Meyer, Stephenie. *Eclipse*. New York: Little, Brown and Company, 2007. pgs. 274-276

3. John 12:42-43, ESV

4. Matthew 10:39, ESV

5. Luke 14:26, ESV

6. ten Boom, Corrie, John Sherrill, and Elizabeth Sherrill. *The Hiding Place*. Old Tappan, NJ: Bantam Books, 1974. pgs. 233-234

7. Ephesians 2:8-9, ESV

8. Matthew 16:24-25, ESV

Chapter 3

1. Szasz, Thomas. Brainy Quote.com. Quotes. Accessed February 11, 2013.

http://www.brainyquote.com/quotes/quotes/t/thom
asszas155759.html
2. Dictionary.com. Dictionary (narcissism). Accessed February 11, 2013.
http://dictionary.reference.com/browse/narcissism?s=t.
3. MayoClinic.com. Health Information (Narcissistic Personality Disorder Symptoms). Accessed February 11, 2013.
http://www.mayoclinic.com/health/narcissistic-personality-disorder/DS00652/DSECTION=symptoms.
4. Dictionary.com. Quotes (Mason Cooley). Accessed February 11, 2013.
http://quotes.dictionary.com/the_narcissist_enjoys_being_looked_at_and_not.
5. MayoClinic.com. Health Information (Narcissistic Personality Disorder Causes). Accessed February 11, 2013.
http://www.mayoclinic.com/health/narcissistic-personality-disorder/DS00652/DSECTION=causes.
6. MayoClinic.com. Health Information (Narcissistic Personality Disorder Causes). Accessed February 11, 2013.
http://www.mayoclinic.com/health/narcissistic-personality-disorder/DS00652/DSECTION=causes.
7. Tozer, A.W. *The Pursuit of God*. 1948. Project Gutenberg (EBook #25141).
8. Meyer, Stephenie. *New Moon*. 1st Paperback Ed. New York: Little, Brown and Company, 2008. pg. 527

9. Tozer, A.W. *The Pursuit of God*. 1948. Project Gutenberg (EBook #25141).
10. Tozer, A.W. *The Pursuit of God*. 1948. Project Gutenberg (EBook #25141).
11. Ephesians 4:22-24 ESV
12. Ephesians 5:8-10, ESV
13. 2 Corinthians 5:17, ESV
14. Galatians 5:17, ESV
15. Romans 3:10-18, ESV
16. 2 Corinthians 3:18, ESV
17. Isaiah 55:8-9, ESV

Chapter 4

1. Picoult, Jodi. *My Sister's Keeper*. New York: Washington Square Press, 2004. pg. 158
2. Revelation 12:12, ESV
3. Revelation 12:7-9, ESV
4. Goodreads.com. William Shakespeare Quotes (King Lear). Accessed February 11, 2013. http://www.goodreads.com/quotes/86616-the-prince-of-darkness-is-a-gentleman.
5. 2 Corinthians 11:14, ESV
6. John 8:44b, ESV

Chapter 5

1. Meyer, Stephenie. *Twilight*. 1st Media Tie-in Ed. New York: Little, Brown and Company, 2008. pg. 302
2. Meyer, Stephenie. *Twilight*. 1st Media Tie-in Ed. New York: Little, Brown and Company, 2008. pgs. 273-274

3. Meyer, Stephenie. *Twilight.* 1st Media Tie-in Ed. New York: Little, Brown and Company, 2008. pg. 302

4. Deuteronomy 4:24, ESV

5. Hosea 2:13, NKJV

6. 2 Kings 23:25, ESV

7. Matthew 22:37, ESV

8. Dictionary.com. Dictionary (all). Accessed February 11, 2013. http;//dictionary.reference.com/browse/all?s=t.

Chapter 6

1. Hugo, Victor. *Les Misérables.* New York: Penguin Books, 1982. pg. 104

2. Hugo, Victor. *Les Misérables.* 1862. Project Gutenberg (EBook #135).

3. Hugo, Victor. *Les Misérables.* 1862. Project Gutenberg (EBook #135).

4. Hugo, Victor. *Les Misérables.* New York: Penguin Books, 1982. pg. 104

5. Hugo, Victor. *Les Misérables.* 1862. Project Gutenberg (EBook #135).

6. Hugo, Victor. *Les Misérables.* New York: Penguin Books, 1982. pg. 115

7. Hugo, Victor. *Les Misérables.* 1862. Project Gutenberg (EBook #135).

8. Hugo, Victor. *Les Misérables.* New York: Penguin Books, 1982. pg. 770

Chapter 7

1. Niffenegger, Audrey. *The Time Traveler's Wife.* Orlando: Harcourt Books, 2003. pg. 326

2. Proverbs 4:23, ESV

3. BibleStudyTools.com. Old Testament Hebrew Lexicon (lebab). Accessed February 11, 2013. http://www.biblestudytools.com/lexicons/hebrew/nas/lebab.html.

4. LatinWordTranslation.com. cor. Accessed February 11, 2013. http://www.latinwordtranslation.com/1/heart.

5. Dictionary.com. Dictionary (core). Accessed February 11, 2013. http://dictionary.reference.com/browse/core?s=t.

6. Luke 10:38-40a, ESV

7. Luke 10:40b-42, ESV

8. Psalm 90:14, ESV

9. Ecclesiastes 2:11b, ESV

10. Ecclesiastes 1:1-11, ESV

11. Research obtained through a series of e-mails from Dr. Wayne Esaias at Goddard Space Flight Center and A. Mortensen at the University of Florida, Department of Entomology and Nematology.

12. Amos 4:6, ESV

13. Isaiah 55:1-3, ESV

Chapter 8

1. Meyer, Stephenie. *Breaking Dawn.* New York: Little, Brown and Company, 2008. pg. 24

2. Meyer, Stephenie. *Twilight*. 1st Media Tie-in Ed. New York: Little, Brown and Company, 2008. pg. 229

3. Magee, David, and Simon Beaufoy. *Miss Pettigrew Lives For A Day*. DVD. Directed by Bharat Nalluri. 2008. Universal City: Universal Studios.

4. Psalm 139:1-18, ESV

5. Genesis 1:27, ESV

6. Tozer, A.W. *The Pursuit of God*. 1948. Project Gutenberg (EBook #25141).

7. 1 Corinthians 2:10-12, ESV

8. Dorman, Douglas. "It's Not About You." *Your Next Step Ministries, Daily Walk* (December 1, 2011).

9. Heller, Jennifer, and David Heller. *You Would Love Me Too*. Butter Lid Publishing, 2009.

Chapter 9

1. McKinley, Robin. *The Blue Sword*. New York: Ace Books, 1987. pg. 8

2. Dictionary.com. Dictionary (ennui). Accessed February 11, 2013. http://dictionary.reference.com/browse/ennui?s=t

3. Merriam-Webster.com. Dictionary (satiety). Accessed February 11, 2013. http://www.merriam-webster.com/dictionary/satiety.

4. Dictionary.com. Dictionary (romantic). Accessed February 11, 2013. http://dictionary.reference.com/browse/romantic?s=t.

5. Dictionary.com. Dictionary (adventure). Accessed February 11, 2013. http://dictionary.reference.com/browse/adventure?s=t.

6. Dictionary.com. Dictionary (excite). Accessed February 11, 2013. http://dictionary.reference.com/browse/excite?s=t.

7. Collins, Suzanne. *Mockingjay.* New York: Scholastic Press, 2010. pg. 90

8. Tolkien, J.R.R. *The Lord of the Rings: The Two Towers.* New York: Houghton Mifflin Company, 1994. pg. 696

9. 1 Kings 17:2-6, ESV

10. Hebrews 11:6, ESV

11. 2 Corinthians 5:15, ESV

12. Esther 2:17, ESV

13. Esther 3:13-14, ESV

14. Esther 4:8b, ESV

15. Esther 4:11, ESV

16. Esther 4:13-14, ESV

17. Esther 4:16, ESV

Made in the USA
Lexington, KY
08 January 2014